CAST IRON
PALEO

101 ONE-PAN RECIPES
FOR QUICK AND DELICIOUS MEALS ...
PLUS HASSLE-FREE CLEANUP

PAMELA ELLGEN

Ulysses Press

Text copyright © 2016 Pamela Ellgen. Design and concept copyright © 2016 Ulysses Press and its licensors. All rights reserved. Any unauthorized duplication in whole or in part or dissemination of this edition by any means (including but not limited to photocopying, electronic devices, digital versions, and the Internet) will be prosecuted to the fullest extent of the law.

Published in the United States by
ULYSSES PRESS
P.O. Box 3440
Berkeley, CA 94703
www.ulyssespress.com

ISBN: 978-1-61243-640-1
Library of Congress Control Number: 2016950669

Printed in Canada by Marquis Book Printing

10 9 8 7 6 5 4 3 2 1

Acquisitions Editor: Bridget Thoreson
Managing Editor: Claire Chun
Project Editor: Alice Riegert
Editor: Renee Rutledge
Proofreader: Shayna Keyles
Production: Caety Klingman
Front cover design: Michelle Thompson
Cover photographs: Pamela Ellgen

Distributed by Publishers Group West

To my husband, Rich, for your love and for always doing the dishes.

Contents

Introduction

I would love to tell you that I grew up watching my grandmother cook on a cast iron skillet while I played on the kitchen floor, unwittingly picking up the secrets to perfect cast iron cooking. I wish I could tell you that she passed along her well-seasoned cast iron skillet to me when I got married.

But it was the 1980s, full of low-fat foods, nonstick cookware, and aerobics videos. I may or may not have embraced all of those!

I didn't learn the secrets of cast iron cooking until I was an adult and had been cooking for several years. I wanted the ease of nonstick cookware (without the toxic effects of the coating) coupled with the superior browning produced by my expensive stainless steel pans. I also wanted cookware that I could easily transfer from stove top to oven and back.

The cast iron skillet offered all of the features I wanted. It quickly became my go-to pan for perfectly seared meats, flavorful casseroles, and rustic stews. It also simplified Paleo cooking, which can easily become more elaborate than a menu built on meat and vegetables ever should be. One pan brought me back to the elemental principles of the Paleo movement and served up some delicious meals in the process.

Someday when I have grandchildren, I intend to pass my culinary wisdom and recipes along to them, but they'll have to pry the skillet out of my hands.

CHAPTER ONE

Cast Iron Cooking

Whether you've been cooking with cast iron for decades or your skillet still has the price tag on the bottom, here's everything you need to know about cast iron cooking plus a little history on this essential kitchen tool.

History of Cast Iron Cookware

The widespread use of iron came around 2,000 BC, long after the original Paleo diet had faded into obscurity. Even then, it was predominantly used in making tools and weapons. The first evidence of cast iron cookware appeared between 200 BC and 200 AD in China, where cast iron pans were used for salt evaporation. It has been used since then in kitchens around the globe. In Japan, teapots made of cast iron, called *tetsubin*, are heated over a charcoal fire and have been used as early as 1500. In the Netherlands, special techniques using sand to create a smooth, enameled cast iron cookware surface emerged around 1600. The English observed this improved method for making pots and copied the technique in the 1700s, resulting in what has since been called the "Dutch oven." Cast iron cookware became a staple in European and colonial American kitchens thereafter. In the 1900s, cast iron was upstaged by steel and aluminum cookware, but cast iron aficionados remained loyal, and for good reason.

Benefits of Cast Iron Cookware

Cast iron pans offer numerous advantages over other cooking vessels, including excellent heat retention, a nonstick surface, affordability, and durability.

Cast iron pans retain and transmit heat well. By preheating the pan for a few minutes, you can generate a very hot surface useful for producing an excellent sear on meats. This is important because you don't want a pan's temperature to drop precipitously when you add food, especially if you're trying to sauté vegetables or brown meat.

Well-seasoned cast iron skillets are also naturally nonstick, making them a good option for eggs, paella, and other foods that tend to adhere to cooking surfaces. Conventional nonstick cookware cannot be preheated without damaging the surface of the pan and generating a slew of chemicals into the air, and they don't produce a good sear. Cast iron offers both nonstick and superior browning capabilities.

Cast iron pans are also inexpensive, especially when compared to high-end cookware used by professional chefs. You might already have a cast iron skillet in your attic or be able to pick one up at a garage sale. Because the pan is a solid piece of metal, it is virtually indestructible and can last for generations.

Cast iron cooking also imparts the mineral iron into foods. For some individuals, particularly premenopausal women, this is a desirable feature. However, if you're following a Paleo diet and eating plenty of red meat and organ meats, you may already have ample iron stores.

How to Choose a Cast Iron Skillet

You can find cast iron cookware ranging in price from less than $20 to well over $200. The differences will be more apparent depending

on your level of experience working with the cast iron skillet and your expectations of the pan. Some features to consider:

Size

Choose a cast iron skillet that is about the same size as your heat source, especially if you're cooking on an electric stove. A skillet that overhangs by a few inches on each side, especially if it is a less-expensive model, will not transmit heat throughout the pan as well and may have hot spots. For the recipes in this book, I used a 12-inch skillet.

Finish

Cast iron skillets with an enamel finish do not require preseasoning and are easier to clean. Enamel is also nonreactive, so tomato and other acidic sauces do not leach metallic flavors into the food.

Enamel does not retain the flavors of years of seasoning and doesn't offer the same level of nonstick capacity of unenameled cast iron. Enameled cast iron also doesn't impart iron to the foods, which may or may not be a desirable feature.

Price

If you're eager to get started without a significant investment, go for an economical pan. Lodge makes inexpensive cast iron skillets that are available online and in most home goods stores such as Target and Walmart. Le Creuset and Staub offer more expensive cast iron cookware in a wide variety of sizes and attractive finishes. They are available online and in fine cooking stores, such as Sur la Table and Williams-Sonoma.

Ergonomics

The cast iron skillet is heavy and may require two hands (not to mention pot holders) to move from stove top to oven. Two ergonomic handles can make this easier.

Seasoning Your Cast Iron Skillet

If you choose an enamel-finish cast iron pan, no seasoning is required. However, if your pan has a matte black finish, you should season it before your first use and plan your first few recipes to be high-fat, low-acid dishes without potent flavors, such as fish.

1. Remove stickers from the pan and wash with hot, soapy water to remove dust and residue. Rinse and thoroughly dry with a towel.

2. Coat the inside and outside of the skillet with a neutral flavored oil, such as palm shortening, macadamia oil, or avocado oil.

3. Place the skillet upside down in a preheated 325°F oven, setting a sheet of aluminum foil on the bottom rack of the oven to catch any drops of oil.

4. Bake for one hour and then turn off the heat. Allow the skillet to cool in the oven.

5. Wipe the exterior of the skillet with a paper towel to remove any extra oil.

6. It is now ready to use.

Caring for Your Cast Iron Skillet

Enamel-finished skillets can be cleaned in the same way you clean your other cookware, by hand with hot soapy water.

Seasoned cast iron skillets should not be cleaned with dish soap because it strips the seasoning and oils from the pan. Instead use hot water and a kitchen scrub brush. For stuck-on pieces of food, use a teaspoon of coarse salt and a paper towel to scrub it away. Dry thoroughly inside and out before storing the cast iron skillet to prevent rust. After the first several uses, rub the inside of the clean skillet with a few drops of oil while it is still warm from cleaning before you put it away.

CHAPTER TWO

Paleo Diet Basics

The Paleo diet is based on the premise that the foods that humans ate for 99 percent of our evolutionary history—the time before the advent of agriculture—should comprise most, if not all, of our diet today. This includes things that could have been hunted or gathered: wild game and fish, roots, vegetables, seasonal fruit, eggs, nuts, and seeds. The Paleo diet confers numerous health benefits as well, which is not surprising since it eliminates the refined carbohydrates that dominate the Western diet. People who adopt a Paleo diet often observe weight loss, reduced food cravings, better sleep, elimination of allergies, improved skin clarity, better digestive function, and even remission of autoimmune disorders.

What to Eat

Modern interpretations of the hunter gatherer diet include pastured meats, wild fish and seafood, locally grown seasonal produce, nuts, seeds, fermented foods, and healthy fats, such as coconut and olive oils. These foods are loaded with the essential fats, amino acids, digestible carbohydrates, fiber, vitamins, minerals, antioxidants, and phytochemicals that have contributed to health and longevity for millennia.

Meat and Poultry

Meat and poultry form the caloric foundation of the Paleo diet. Wild game and organic, pastured meats are ideal. While none of the recipes in this book explicitly call for grass-fed, organic, free-range, or pastured meats, those are the best choices.

If that is not possible, choose meat that has not been fed animal byproducts or administered routine antibiotics or hormones. For nutrition and flavor, choose fatty cuts of meat, such as chicken thighs over chicken breasts. Better yet, buy the whole chicken and use the bones to make a nourishing bone broth. Organ meats are also a rich source of minerals and should occasionally grace your table. Here are the more common meat and poultry options in the Paleo diet:

- Beef
- Bison
- Chicken
- Duck
- Lamb

- Organ meats
- Pork
- Quail
- Turkey
- Venison

Fish and Seafood

Choose wild seafood over farmed, except in the case of shellfish, such as mussels and oysters. To avoid excess mercury exposure, choose fish at the bottom of the food chain and only occasionally eat predators such as shark and tuna. Here are the more common seafood options in the Paleo diet:

- Abalone
- Anchovies
- Clams
- Cod
- Halibut
- Mussels
- Oysters

- Salmon
- Sardines
- Scallops
- Sea Bass
- Shrimp
- Snapper
- Trout

Vegetables

The healthiest approach to Paleo includes loads of non-starchy vegetables. Choose locally grown, organic produce whenever possible and avoid canned vegetables, which are bereft of nutritional value. (I make an exception for canned tomatoes, technically a fruit.) Here are the more common vegetable options in the Paleo diet:

- Acorn squash
- Artichokes
- Asparagus
- Bell peppers
- Broccoli
- Brussels sprouts
- Butternut squash
- Cabbage
- Cauliflower
- Collard greens
- Cucumbers
- Eggplants
- Endive
- Fennel
- Green beans
- Kohlrabi
- Leeks
- Mushrooms
- Onions
- Peas
- Pumpkin
- Radicchio
- Radishes
- Snow peas
- Spinach
- Swiss chard
- Watercress
- Zucchini

Root vegetables, often called "starchy tubers," are a great source of carbohydrates in an otherwise low-carb diet. Potatoes are a gray area in Paleo because of their high glycemic index and the saponins in potato skins. However, many Paleo diet proponents recommend them because they provide resistant starch when cooked and cooled and are a good source of energy. I have included them sparingly in this book, knowing that some people choose to avoid them. Use sweet potatoes in their place if you wish.

Here are some of the more common varieties of root vegetables in the Paleo diet:

- Carrots
- Potatoes
- Rutabagas
- Sweet potatoes
- Turnips

Fruit

Fruit provides a delicious accent to the Paleo diet but ideally should be locally grown, in season, and consumed in moderation, especially for people who are trying to lose weight. Avocado and tomato are typically considered vegetables and do not contain the same amount of fructose and glucose present in sweet fruits. Here are the more common fruit options in the Paleo diet:

- Apples
- Avocados
- Blackberries
- Blueberries
- Cantaloupe
- Citrus fruits
- Figs
- Grapes
- Mango
- Nectarines
- Peaches
- Pears
- Plums
- Raspberries
- Rhubarb
- Strawberries
- Tomatoes
- Watermelon
- Root Vegetables

Nuts and Seeds

Nuts and seeds are great for sprinkling on salads, snacking, and using in Paleo baked goods. To improve their digestibility, soak nuts and seeds in fresh water overnight, rinse and drain thoroughly, and add to the desired recipe. To make them dry and crisp, spread the soaked nuts on a tray and place in a dehydrator or warmed oven until crisp. Drying times vary significantly depending on the type of nut.

Peanuts are not a nut but a legume and are thus not part of the Paleo diet. While they do have a similar macronutrient profile to tree nuts, such as almonds, they may cause digestive discomfort and are not included in this book.

Here are some of the more common varieties of nuts in the Paleo diet:

- Almonds
- Brazil nuts
- Cashews
- Macadamia nuts
- Pistachios
- Sesame seeds
- Sunflower seeds
- Walnuts

Healthy Fats

I prefer to use refined coconut oil in high-heat cooking because it stands up well to the heat and does not impart a coconut flavor to the food. Sometimes that is desirable, such as with the Coconut-Crusted Plantain Tacos (page 58), but I don't want all of my food to taste like coconut. I only use extra-virgin olive oil in raw preparations, such as salad dressings, and sometimes in low to moderate heat cooking with the cast iron skillet.

Avocado and macadamia oils have a more neutral flavor than olive oil and are especially useful in making mayonnaise and aioli. Ghee is clarified butter and has a deliciously buttery aroma and flavor. However, some people are especially sensitive to dairy, so I provide alternatives whenever I call for it in a recipe.

- Avocado oil
- Coconut oil
- Ghee
- Macadamia oil
- Extra-virgin olive oil

Fermented Foods

Fermentation occurs in nature and has been part of the human diet since the beginning. Fermented foods are present in most cultures and offer a friendly boost to the gut microbiome. Make your own ferments or purchase them from the store. Soybeans are a legume and thus not technically Paleo. However, fermenting soy improves its digestibility. I include it sparingly in this book. If you prefer, use coconut aminos instead of soy sauce when called for in a recipe. Here are just a few of the most common fermented foods:

- Kimchi
- Kombucha
- Miso
- Pickles

- Preserved lemons
- Sauerkraut
- Soy sauce
- Yogurt

What Not to Eat

Noticeably absent from the menu are grains, legumes, dairy, refined sugar, and processed foods.

Grains and Legumes

Grains, particularly wheat and corn, comprise the vast majority of the Standard American Diet, which isn't surprising since grains were placed at the foundation of the food pyramid by the USDA. Processed grains in the form of wheat bread, bagels, and cereals took the place of healthful fats during the last half of the twentieth century, when the low-fat diet dogma took hold. Unfortunately, overconsumption of grains, namely wheat, and added sugars has had devastating effects on public health. They elevate blood sugar and insulin, contributing to diabetes, heart disease, and a host of other chronic and degenerative diseases, not the least of which is obesity. Legumes also elevate blood sugar, though not as dramatically as grains.

Both grains and legumes contain naturally occurring chemicals that make them difficult to digest and contribute to a permeable gut membrane, which may trigger autoimmune disorders.

Dairy

Cow's milk contains proteins and sugars that many adults find difficult to digest and are causative of allergic reactions. However, some Paleo proponents suggest after an elimination period that full-fat dairy products should be re-introduced to determine tolerance. The first to try is ghee, which is pure butterfat clarified to remove lactose, casein, or whey. Other options include heavy cream, butter, full-fat yogurt, and some cheeses.

Refined Sugar

Refined sugar in all its forms (white sugar, brown sugar, and high-fructose corn syrup) is not on the Paleo table. It has destructive effects on blood sugar levels, insulin production, weight control, inflammation, and mental health, not to mention its addictive nature. Many people in the Paleo community consider honey, maple syrup, and coconut palm sugar acceptable forms of sugar. I have included a chapter of desserts featuring these sweeteners in modest amounts, but I think it's important to remember that hunter gatherers don't eat salted caramel cupcakes made with almond flour and maple syrup and dusted with fleur de sel.

Processed Foods

Processed foods—the foods that comprise the majority of the average grocery store—are not on the Paleo menu. Processed food is any food that has been deconstructed, pulverized, concentrated, and reassembled into something completely unlike the original food in nutritional value. Michael Pollan calls these "edible food like substances."

Serving Sizes

In this book I offer a range of serving sizes. Clearly, a middle-aged man with a sedentary occupation consumes far less than a young woman who cycles to work and spends her weekends competing in triathlons. To gauge the correct serving size for you, glance at the ingredients and compare them to the portions you typically eat. When a recipe is labeled "Serves 2 to 4," it is intended to feed two moderately active adults and two children.

CHAPTER THREE

Breakfast

VEGETABLE GARDEN HASH

Cut up all of the vegetables the night before to make breakfast preparation a breeze. I like to alternate the veggies based on whatever is in season or, truthfully, whatever is in my fridge and needs to get used. Serve with a couple of fried eggs, which you can make in the same pan in minutes after the vegetables are done.

SERVES: 2   PREP TIME: 10 minutes   COOK TIME: 15 to 20 minutes

2 tablespoons coconut oil, divided

1 sweet potato, peeled and cut into ½-inch cubes

pinch red chili flakes

½ red onion, halved and thinly sliced

¼ fennel bulb, thinly sliced

1 small zucchini, diced

1 cup halved mushrooms

1 clove garlic, minced

sea salt to taste

freshly ground pepper to taste

4 fried eggs (optional)

1. Heat 1 tablespoon of the coconut oil in the cast iron skillet over medium heat. When it is hot, add the sweet potato and red chili flakes. Season lightly with salt. Cook for 5 minutes until the sweet potato is browned on all sides.

2. Push the sweet potato to the sides of the pan and add the onion and fennel. Season lightly with salt and cook until they have picked up some color and are beginning to soften, about 5 minutes.

3. Push the onion and fennel to the sides of the pan and add the remaining tablespoon of oil. Cook the zucchini and mushrooms for 3 to 5 minutes until just browned.

4. Stir all of the ingredients together and add the garlic. Cook for another minute. Season with salt and pepper and serve along with 4 fried eggs, if desired.

SAUSAGE AND SWEET POTATO HASH

Sometimes I get tired of bacon and eggs for breakfast and like to switch things up with spicy Italian sausage and sweet potatoes. Choose the best quality sausage you can find or make your own using ground pork, crushed fennel seed, red chili flakes, and a splash of red wine vinegar. For a milder flavor, use chicken and apple sausage.

SERVES: 2   PREP TIME: 10 minutes   COOK TIME: 20 minutes

2 mild or hot Italian sausages, casings removed

2 sweet potatoes, peeled and cut into ½-inch cubes

½ red onion, halved and thinly sliced

sea salt to taste

freshly ground pepper to taste

2 fried eggs (optional)

1. Heat the cast iron skillet over medium heat. When it is hot, crumble the sausages into the pan. Cook for 5 minutes until it is gently browned and barely cooked through. Use a slotted spoon to remove it to a separate dish.

2. Add the sweet potatoes to the pan. Season lightly with salt and pepper, and cook until they are browned and nearly soft, about 10 minutes.

3. Add the onion to the pan and cook for 5 minutes until browned and soft.

4. Return the sausages to the pan and give everything a good toss. Adjust seasoning and cook for another minute or two just to integrate the flavors. Serve with 2 fried eggs, if desired.

PLANTAIN, BACON, AND FENNEL HASH

I've been hooked on plantains since I enjoyed them on my birthday after a morning of surfing. My husband Rich and I popped into a sunny Caribbean restaurant in Venice, California, and enjoyed our brunch in the open-air café with endless coffee.

SERVES: 4   PREP TIME: 5 minutes   COOK TIME: 20 minutes

4 slices applewood-smoked bacon, roughly chopped

2 green plantains, sliced ¼-inch thick on a bias

½ fennel bulb, cored and very thinly sliced

pinch red chili flakes

2 cloves garlic, smashed

sea salt to taste

freshly ground pepper taste

4 fried eggs (optional)

1. Cook the bacon in the cast iron skillet over medium-low heat for about 10 minutes, or until the bacon is cooked through and has rendered most of its fat. Remove it with a slotted spoon to a separate dish.

2. Fry the plantain slices in the bacon fat for about 2 to 3 minutes on each side, until well browned. Push them to the sides of the pan.

3. Add the sliced fennel and red chili flakes to the skillet and cook for about 5 minutes, until soft and gently browned. Add the garlic and cook for another minute.

4. Return the bacon to the pan and give everything a good toss. Season with salt and pepper. Serve immediately or transfer to a mortar and pestle and grind into a soft mash. Enjoy it with 4 fried eggs, if desired.

ARTICHOKE AND LEEK FRITTATA

This meatless breakfast entrée makes a delicious addition to brunch or even a light dinner served with a simple salad of mixed greens.

SERVES: 4   PREP TIME: 5 minutes   COOK TIME: 25 minutes

1 tablespoon extra-virgin olive oil

1 cup canned artichoke hearts, drained

1 leek, white and pale green parts only, halved, cleaned, and thinly sliced

1 teaspoon minced fresh thyme leaves

8 eggs, whisked

¼ teaspoon sea salt

1. Preheat the oven to 350°F.

2. Heat the olive oil in the cast iron skillet over medium-high heat. Brown the artichoke hearts for about 5 minutes. Push them to the sides of the pan.

3. Add the leek and thyme, and continue cooking for another 5 minutes.

4. Season the eggs with salt and pour the mixture over the artichoke and leeks. Cook for another 2 minutes on the stove and then transfer to the oven.

5. Bake until the top is set, about 10 to 12 minutes.

BACON AND TOMATO FRITTATA

Think "bacon meets tomato ginger jam" in this sweet and savory one-skillet breakfast.

SERVES: 4   PREP TIME: 5 minutes   COOK TIME: 25 minutes

4 slices applewood-smoked bacon, cut into lardons

1 pint grape tomatoes, halved

1 teaspoon minced ginger

1 clove garlic, minced

1/8 teaspoon red chili flakes

1 teaspoon minced fresh thyme leaves

sea salt to taste

freshly ground pepper to taste

2 teaspoons maple syrup

8 eggs, whisked

1. Preheat the oven to 350°F.

2. Cook the bacon pieces in the cast iron skillet over medium-low heat until they have rendered most of their fat but are not crisp. Use a slotted spoon to remove the bacon to a separate dish.

3. Add the tomatoes, ginger, garlic, red chili flakes, and thyme to the pan. Season with salt and pepper and cook for about 10 minutes, until the tomatoes are soft and fragrant. Add the maple syrup and cook for another minute.

4. Return the bacon to the pan and pour in the eggs.

5. Cook for another 2 minutes on the stove and then transfer to the oven.

6. Bake until the top is set, about 10 to 12 minutes.

HOMEMADE CHICKEN APPLE SAUSAGE

A simple solution for finding healthy sausages is to make your own. Okay, it's not as simple as picking up a package, but it sure beats downing monosodium glutamate and sodium erythorbate with your morning meal. Serve with eggs or use as a filling for omelets or baked acorn squash, or with zucchini noodles.

YIELDS 1 pound   PREP TIME: 5 minutes   COOK TIME: 10 minutes

4 boneless chicken thighs, about 4 ounces each

½ cup dried apples, finely chopped

1 shallot, minced

1 teaspoon minced fresh thyme leaves

¼ teaspoon sea salt

¼ teaspoon freshly ground pepper

1. Process the chicken thighs through the meat-grinder attachment of your stand mixer. Alternatively, purchase ground chicken.

2. Combine the ground chicken with the apples, shallot, thyme, salt, and pepper in a small mixing bowl.

3. Heat the cast iron skillet over medium heat. Crumble the sausage into the pan. Alternately, shape the sausage mixture into 6 individual patties. Cook for a total of 10 minutes, until gently browned and cooked through.

SUN-DRIED TOMATOES VARIATION: Swap the apples for ½ cup of drained sun-dried tomatoes and add 1 teaspoon of minced fresh rosemary and 1 teaspoon of minced garlic.

HOW TO PREPARE ACORN SQUASH: Preheat the oven to 350°F. Slice the acorn squash in half vertically. Scoop out the seeds and strings, and discard. Add ¼ cup of water to a baking dish and place the squash halves cut-side down in the dish. Bake for 40 minutes, or until soft.

ZUCCHINI CARROT HASH BROWNS

For a lower carb and super flavorful version of your favorite breakfast side dish, try these simple hash browns.

SERVES: 2 to 4   PREP TIME: 5 minutes   COOK TIME: 10 minutes

3 medium carrots

2 medium zucchini

1 yellow onion, halved and very thinly sliced

2 tablespoons coconut oil

sea salt to taste

freshly ground pepper to taste

1. Grate the carrots and zucchini using a food processor or box grater and thoroughly squeeze out excess moisture using your hands. Combine the carrots, zucchini, and onion in a mixing bowl.

2. Heat the coconut oil in the cast iron skillet over medium heat.

3. When the pan is hot, sprinkle the vegetables into the pan and season with salt and pepper.

4. Cook for at least 5 minutes, until a brown crust forms on the bottom. Flip the vegetables to brown on the other side, being careful not to stir too much. Cook for another 5 minutes, until gently browned. Serve immediately.

BELL PEPPER VARIATION: Use red or green bell pepper in place of the carrots.

PANCETTA STEWED COLLARDS WITH FRIED EGGS AND ESPRESSO AIOLI

Combine all of the essential breakfast flavors in one pan in this savory breakfast number inspired by the Los Angeles restaurant Egg Slut.

SERVES: 4   PREP TIME: 5 minutes   COOK TIME: 20 minutes

4 eggs, plus 1 egg yolk

1 teaspoon lemon juice

1 tablespoon espresso or very strong coffee

½ cup avocado or macadamia oil

4 ounces diced pancetta

1 bunch collards, ribs removed and sliced into thin ribbons

sea salt to taste

freshly ground pepper to taste

1. Start by making the espresso aioli. Combine the egg yolk, lemon juice, and espresso in a small warmed bowl. Whisk until thoroughly integrated. Slowly drizzle in the oil a few drops at a time, whisking constantly until all of the oil is added and the sauce is thick. Set aside.

2. Cook the pancetta in the cast iron skillet over medium-low heat until it has rendered most of its fat, about 8 to 10 minutes.

3. Add the collard greens to the pan. Season with salt and pepper. Cook until just wilted, about 2 minutes. Transfer the greens and pancetta to individual serving plates.

4. Raise the heat to medium. Crack the eggs into the pan and fry for 5 minutes, or until the whites are set and the yolks are still vibrant yellow. Set one egg atop each bed of greens. Drizzle with the espresso aioli.

CREPES

Given its naturally nonstick surface, the cast iron skillet is the perfect pan for making crepes. Omit the vanilla extract for savory crepes.

YIELDS: 12 crepes   PREP TIME: 5 minutes   COOK TIME: 15 minutes

6 eggs

¾ cup almond milk

1 teaspoon vanilla extract

2 tablespoons coconut flour

1 tablespoon tapioca starch

¼ teaspoon sea salt

1 teaspoon coconut oil, plus more as needed

1. Combine the eggs, almond milk, and vanilla in a blender. Blend for 1 to 2 seconds.

2. Add the coconut flour, tapioca starch, and sea salt. Pulse once or twice and then scrape down the sides. Blend until smooth. Set the batter aside for at least 5 minutes to allow the coconut flour and tapioca starch to absorb the liquid.

3. Meanwhile, heat up the cast iron skillet over medium-low heat. Melt one teaspoon of the coconut oil in the pan. Pour about 2 to 3 table-spoons of the crepe batter into the pan and tilt to spread. Cook for about 1 to 2 minutes until set. Flip and cook for another 30 seconds. Transfer to a parchment-lined serving platter. Repeat with the remaining batter, using additional coconut oil as needed.

CHOCOLATE ALMOND BUTTER CREPES: Prepare the basic crepe recipe as directed. Combine ½ cup almond butter with 2 tablespoons good-quality cocoa powder, 2 tablespoons maple syrup, and ¼ tea-spoon sea salt. Spread a couple tablespoons of the almond chocolate mixture over each crepe.

PROSCIUTTO, PEAR, AND ARUGULA CREPES: Prepare the basic crepe recipe, omitting the vanilla extract. Top each crepe with 2 slices of prosciutto and 4 thin slices of pear. Place under a broiler for about 30 seconds to 1 minute, to toast gently. Top with a handful of arugula.

ALMOND CHEESE–STUFFED CREPES WITH BLUEBERRIES: To make the almond cheese, soak 2 cups of blanched almonds in water overnight. Rinse and drain. Combine the almonds with 1 cup of water, a pinch of sea salt, and 1 teaspoon of vanilla extract in a blender and puree until smooth. Place into a nut milk bag and squeeze very gently to expel most of the water. Store in a covered container in the refrigerator until ready to serve. Prepare the basic crepe recipe as directed. Top each crepe with a spoonful of almond cheese and a handful of blueberries.

DUTCH BABIES

Dutch babies rise to a beautiful height and form a delicious golden crust when cooked in a preheated pan, making the cast iron skillet the ideal choice for going from stove top to oven. They're also a convenient way to serve your entire family a batch of pancakes without standing over the stove flipping away.

SERVES: 4   PREP TIME: 5 minutes   COOK TIME: 25 minutes

1 dozen eggs

1 cup unsweetened almond milk

2 tablespoons maple syrup

1 tablespoon vanilla extract

⅓ cup coconut flour

⅓ cup tapioca starch

¼ teaspoon sea salt

2 tablespoons coconut oil

1. Preheat the oven to 400°F.

2. Combine the eggs, almond milk, maple syrup, and vanilla in a blender. Blend until smooth.

3. Add the coconut flour, tapioca starch, and sea salt. Pulse a few times, scrape down the sides with a spatula, and then blend until smooth. Allow the batter to rest for 5 minutes.

4. Heat the coconut oil in the cast iron skillet over medium heat until hot.

5. Pour in the batter and immediately transfer to the oven. Bake for about 25 minutes, until puffy.

SPICED PEAR DUTCH BABIES: Prepare the recipe as directed. After pouring the batter into the pan, arrange pear wedges from 2 pears in a circular pattern in the pan and shower with ¼ teaspoon of freshly ground nutmeg. Bake as directed.

RASPBERRY ORANGE DUTCH BABIES: Prepare the recipe as directed. After pouring the batter into the pan, scatter 1 pint of fresh raspberries over the batter and shower with 1 teaspoon fresh orange zest. Bake as directed.

PANCAKES

We eat a version of these pancakes at least once a week in my house. They're so good, I can use them to bribe my children to go to bed without a hassle. Best part—they're low in sugar so there's no blood sugar rush followed by the crash of traditional pancakes.

SERVES: 2 to 4   PREP TIME: 5 minutes   COOK TIME: 15 minutes

4 eggs

½ cup coconut milk

1 ripe banana

1 tablespoon vanilla extract

½ teaspoon apple cider vinegar

½ cup packed finely ground, blanched almond flour

¼ cup coconut flour

2 tablespoons tapioca starch

½ teaspoon baking soda

¼ teaspoon sea salt

1 to 2 tablespoons coconut oil

1. Combine the eggs, coconut milk, banana, vanilla extract, and apple cider vinegar in a blender. Puree until smooth.

2. Add the almond flour, coconut flour, tapioca starch, baking soda, and sea salt. Pulse a few times, scrape down the sides, and then blend until smooth. Allow the batter to rest for at least 5 minutes.

3. Heat 1 to 2 teaspoons of coconut oil in the cast iron skillet over medium heat. Pour ¼ cup of batter per pancake into the pan. Cook for 2 to 3 minutes until small air bubbles form in the center of each pancake. Flip carefully and cook for 1 minute on the other side. Repeat with the remaining batter, adding additional coconut oil as needed.

BLUEBERRY PANCAKES: Prepare the recipe as directed. Stir in 1 cup of fresh blueberries and 1 teaspoon fresh lemon zest into the batter before cooking.

CHAPTER FOUR

Vegetables

ASPARAGUS LA PLANCHA

Cooking food "a la plancha" is a Spanish technique for grilling foods on a hot plate. The cast iron skillet is the closest approximation of an actual flattop grill and provides uniform, high heat.

SERVES: 2   PREP TIME: 5 minutes   COOK TIME: 5 minutes

1 bunch asparagus, woody ends trimmed

1 tablespoon coconut oil

zest and juice of 1 lemon

sea salt to taste

freshly ground pepper to taste

1. Heat the cast iron skillet over medium-high heat until it is very hot.

2. Use your hands to coat the asparagus spears in the coconut oil. Add them to the hot skillet and sear until browned and heated through, about 4 to 5 minutes.

3. Transfer them to a serving platter and shower with lemon zest and juice, sea salt, and freshly ground pepper.

INGREDIENT TIP: Contrary to popular belief, spindly, pencil-thin asparagus are not the most tender. Choose fat stalks grown in season for this dish and prepare to be amazed.

BRAZILIAN COLLARDS

These collard greens come together quickly and make a delicious side dish for thick cuts of beef.

SERVES: 2 to 4   PREP TIME: 5 minutes   COOK TIME: 2 minutes

2 tablespoons coconut oil

1 bunch collard greens, thinly sliced in ribbons

2 cloves garlic, minced

pinch red chili flakes

juice of 1 lime

sea salt to taste

1. Heat the cast iron skillet over medium-high heat. Allow it to get very hot.

2. Add the coconut oil and allow it to warm for a second. Add the collard greens and sauté until wilted, about 1 to 2 minutes. Add the garlic and red chili flakes, and cook for another 30 seconds.

3. Season with lime juice and salt.

GREEN BEANS WITH CARAMELIZED SHALLOTS

Blanching and shocking vegetables first is a French cooking technique for yielding a tender crisp snap that makes vegetables absolutely delectable. Because they cook in the skillet in mere minutes, they're easy to throw into the pan after cooking a main dish. I love them with the Maple Almond Pork Chops (page 109).

SERVES: 2   PREP TIME: 10 minutes   COOK TIME: 5 to 10 minutes

1 pound green beans, stems removed

1 tablespoon olive oil

1 shallot, thinly sliced vertically

sea salt to taste

freshly ground pepper to taste

1 teaspoon red wine vinegar

1. Prepare an ice water bath in a large bowl.

2. Bring a large pot of salted water to a boil. Cook the green beans for about 2 minutes, until bright green. Use tongs to remove them from the pot and plunge them into the ice water to halt the cooking process. Drain and set aside until you're ready to complete the dish. These steps can be done up to a day in advance.

3. Heat the olive oil in the cast iron skillet over medium heat. (The oil can be omitted or reduced if you're making this dish following another dish containing oil.) Add the shallot to the pan and season with salt. Cook for about 5 minutes until soft and gently browned.

4. Add the green beans to the hot skillet and cook just until heated through. Season with salt and pepper. Splash with the red wine vinegar just before serving.

CARAMELIZED FENNEL AND ORANGE

The flavors in this simple side dish are sweet and savory with a faint anise flavor. To make it a complete meal, remove the fennel and orange to a serving plate, and poach a few halibut filets in the pan sauce.

SERVES: 2 to 4   PREP TIME: 5 minutes   COOK TIME: 20 minutes

2 tablespoons olive oil

1 fennel bulb, cut into 8 to 12 thin wedges, fronds reserved

2 oranges, divided

1 teaspoon sherry vinegar

¼ cup chicken or vegetable broth

sea salt to taste

freshly ground pepper to taste

1. Heat the olive oil in the cast iron skillet over medium-high heat. Add the fennel wedges and sear for 5 minutes. Flip to the other side and brown for another 5 minutes.

2. Use a knife to remove the peel and pith from one orange. Stand the orange on one end and use a paring knife to remove the segments between the membranes. Set them aside. Zest and juice the second orange.

3. Add the orange zest and juice, vinegar, and broth to the skillet. Season with salt and pepper. Continue cooking for about 10 minutes, until the fennel is soft and the liquid has reached a syrupy consistency. Add the orange segments and fennel fronds to the pan before serving.

ROASTED CAULIFLOWER WITH SERRANO, ALMOND, AND PARSLEY PICADA

When I first tested this recipe, I wondered if sherry vinegar, dark chocolate, and parsley could possibly work together. What a delicious surprise—they do!

SERVES: 2 to 4   PREP TIME: 10 minutes   COOK TIME: 35 minutes

2 tablespoons almonds

2 tablespoons extra-virgin olive oil

1 small head cauliflower

¼ cup minced fresh parsley

1 serrano pepper, minced

1 small shallot, thinly sliced

2 teaspoons finely grated dark chocolate

1½ tablespoons sherry vinegar

sea salt to taste

freshly ground pepper to taste

1. Preheat the oven to 375°F.

2. Heat the cast iron skillet over medium-high heat. Toast the almonds in the dry skillet for 2 to 3 minutes until they begin to brown. Transfer the almonds to a mortar and pestle and mash until roughly ground.

3. Add the olive oil to the hot skillet and then add the cauliflower. Toss to coat in the oil and sear for 5 minutes. Transfer the pan to the oven and roast for 25 to 30 minutes, until charred on the bottom and tender.

4. Meanwhile, add the parsley, serrano pepper, shallot, and dark chocolate to the mortar and pestle to make the picada. Stir in the sherry vinegar.

5. Carefully remove the skillet from the oven. Add the picada and toss the cauliflower briefly. Season with salt and pepper. Serve warm or at room temperature.

RATATOUILLE

This Provençal recipe is a staple in my house. I like to serve it as an appetizer or a filling side dish for fish or chicken.

SERVES: 2 to 4   PREP TIME: 10 minutes   COOK TIME: 1 hour

½ cup extra-virgin olive oil, divided

1 eggplant, cut into ½-inch cubes

2 small zucchini, cut into ½-inch pieces

1 medium yellow onion, minced

4 cloves garlic, minced

2 sprigs fresh thyme leaves

1 sprig fresh rosemary, needles minced

1 pint grape tomatoes, halved

2 tablespoons balsamic vinegar

¼ cup roughly chopped fresh basil

sea salt to taste

freshly ground pepper to taste

1. Preheat the oven to 375°F.

2. Heat ¼ cup of the olive oil in the cast iron skillet over medium heat. Fry the eggplant in the oil, tossing to coat. Season with salt and pepper, and cook for about 10 minutes. Transfer to a colander to drain.

3. Add 2 teaspoons oil and the zucchini to the pan, season with salt and pepper, and cook until gently browned, about 5 minutes.

4. Transfer the zucchini to the colander. Add 2 teaspoons oil and the onion, garlic, thyme, and rosemary to the pan, and cook for 5 minutes, until somewhat softened. Add the tomatoes to the pan and cook for another 5 minutes.

5. Return the eggplant and zucchini to the pan, pour in the balsamic vinegar, and give everything a good toss.

6. Roast uncovered for 30 to 40 minutes. Remove from the oven and stir in the fresh basil. Allow to cool for at least 10 minutes before serving.

CHARRED RADISHES WITH OLIVE AIOLI

This recipe is inspired by an appetizer at one of my favorite restaurants in California, Gjelina in Venice. The saltiness of the olives can easily overpower the aioli, so wait until it is prepared to season with salt.

SERVES: 2 to 4   PREP TIME: 5 minutes   COOK TIME: 5 to 7 minutes

1 tablespoon coconut oil

1 bunch radishes, sliced in half lengthwise, with 1 inch of green tops remaining

1 egg yolk

1 teaspoon lemon juice

1 clove garlic

½ cup macadamia or avocado oil

1 tablespoon minced Kalamata olives

sea salt to taste

freshly ground black pepper to taste

1 lemon, cut into wedges

1. Heat the coconut oil in the cast iron skillet over medium-high heat. Sear the radishes, cut-side down until deeply browned, about 5 to 7 minutes. Transfer the radishes to a serving platter. Season with pepper.

2. Meanwhile, combine the egg yolk and lemon juice in a small mixing bowl. Grate the garlic using a Microplane grater to produce a fine puree. Whisk the mixture thoroughly to combine.

3. Continue whisking as you add the oil a few droplets at a time until it is all incorporated. Fold in the Kalamata olives. Season to taste with salt.

4. Serve the aioli alongside the charred radishes and lemon wedges.

PAN-ROASTED ENDIVE WITH PRESERVED LEMONS

I'm in love with preserved lemons, which is convenient because I have a Meyer lemon tree in my backyard that demands some creativity to use up all of its fruit. The brininess of the preserved lemon marries beautifully with grassy parsley and toasted almonds.

SERVES: 2 to 4   PREP TIME: 5 minutes   COOK TIME: 5 to 7 minutes

1½ tablespoons olive oil, divided

4 heads Belgian endive, halved and ends trimmed

1 tablespoon minced preserved lemon

2 tablespoons roughly chopped toasted almonds

1 tablespoon minced fresh flat-leaf parsley

sea salt to taste

freshly ground pepper to taste

1. Heat 1 tablespoon of the olive oil in the cast iron skillet over medium-high heat. Place the endives cut-side down in the skillet and cover with a pizza pan or with a lid allowing some steam to escape. Cook for 5 to 7 minutes, until the bottoms are charred and the vegetable begins to soften.

2. Meanwhile, combine the preserved lemon, almonds, and parsley in a ramekin.

3. Place the endive on a serving platter, cut-side up. Drizzle with the remaining ½ tablespoon of olive oil, top with the lemon mixture, season with salt and pepper, and serve.

CHARRED JERUSALEM ARTICHOKES

Also called sunchokes, Jerusalem artichokes are a root vegetable that does best when cooked over intense heat. A preheated cast iron skillet does the trick.

SERVES: 2 to 4   PREP TIME: 5 minutes   COOK TIME: 10 to 15 minutes

1 pound Jerusalem artichokes, quartered

1 tablespoon coconut oil

sea salt to taste

freshly ground pepper to taste

1. Preheat the oven to 425°F.

2. Heat the cast iron skillet over high heat until very hot.

3. In a medium bowl, toss the Jerusalem artichokes with the coconut oil to coat thoroughly. Season with salt and pepper. Add them to the pan and immediately transfer it to the oven. Roast uncovered for 10 to 15 minutes, until the vegetables are charred and tender.

4. To serve, toss the Jerusalem artichokes with Pistachio Mint Pesto.

PISTACHIO MINT PESTO

Mint and pistachio bring lively new flavors to the classic pesto made with basil. It is delicious on the preceding recipe for Jerusalem Artichokes as well as on roasted lamb.

YIELDS: ½ cup   PREP TIME: 5 minutes   COOK TIME: 0 minutes

2 tablespoons roughly chopped pistachios

¼ cup roughly chopped fresh mint

1 shallot, minced

3 tablespoons extra-virgin olive oil

1 teaspoon red wine vinegar

Combine the pistachios, mint, shallot, and olive oil in a mortar and pestle or small food processor. Grind into a chunky paste. Add the red wine vinegar just before serving.

PAN-ROASTED CARROTS AND ONIONS

The heat of the cast iron skillet caramelizes the carrots and onions for a decadent vegetable side dish.

SERVES: 2 to 4   PREP TIME: 10 minutes   COOK TIME: 30 minutes

1 bunch carrots, with tops

2 tablespoons coconut oil

½ red onion, thinly sliced in wedges

sea salt to taste

freshly ground pepper to taste

1. Preheat the oven to 375°F.

2. Remove the carrot tops, leaving about 1 inch of the stem on the carrots. Reserve the greens for the Carrot Top Pesto (recipe follows). Slice the carrots in half lengthwise.

3. Heat the cast iron skillet over high heat for 4 minutes, until very hot. Add the coconut oil. Place the carrots and onion into the pan, and toss gently to coat in the oil. Try to push the carrots so that the cut sides are touching the pan. They will not all fit in one layer. Season with salt and pepper. Place the pan in the oven and roast uncovered for 30 minutes.

4. To serve, drizzle with the Carrot Top Pesto.

CARROT TOP PESTO

Carrot Top Pesto is my new obsession. The flavor of the greens is herbaceous and subtle, and it just makes sense, in that "stem to root" sort of way when you have a beautiful bunch of carrots from the farmer's market.

YIELDS ¾ cup   PREP TIME: 5 minutes   COOK TIME: 0 minutes

1 bunch carrot tops	1 small clove garlic
⅓ cup extra-virgin olive oil	1 tablespoon lemon juice
¼ teaspoon sea salt	

1. Discard the tough stems from your carrot tops and thoroughly rinse the greens. It should yield about ½ cup packed greens.

2. Add the olive oil, sea salt, and garlic. Puree with an immersion blender until smooth.

3. Stir in the lemon juice just before serving.

PAN-ROASTED ROMANESCO

I love the texture of cauliflower, but sometimes I want a little color on my plate. Enter, Romanesco. It has a gorgeous chartreuse hue, a crunchy texture, and nutty flavor.

SERVES: 2 to 4   PREP TIME: 5 minutes   COOK TIME: 20 to 25 minutes

1 head Romanesco, broken into florets

1 tablespoon coconut oil

sea salt to taste

freshly ground pepper to taste

1 tablespoon minced fresh parsley

zest and juice of 1 lemon

1. Preheat the oven to 375°F.

2. Heat the cast iron skillet over high heat until very hot.

3. In a medium bowl, toss the Romanesco with the coconut oil to coat thoroughly. Season with salt and pepper. Add to the pan and immediately transfer it to the oven.

4. Roast uncovered for 20 to 25 minutes, until the vegetables are charred and tender.

5. To serve, toss with the parsley, lemon zest, and lemon juice.

SMOKY STEWED KALE WITH DATES

The sweetness of the dates in this smoky stewed kale dish nearly pushes it into the dessert category, especially if you don't eat sweets. It's the ultimate kale delivery method for the kale haters out there.

SERVES: 2 to 4   PREP TIME: 5 minutes   COOK TIME: 25 minutes

4 slices applewood-smoked bacon, cut into lardons

1 red onion, thinly sliced

2 medjool dates, pitted and roughly chopped

1 bunch kale, ribs minced, leaves roughly chopped

½ cup chicken broth

1 tablespoon red wine vinegar

sea salt to taste

freshly ground pepper to taste

1. Cook the bacon in the cast iron skillet over medium-low heat until it renders most of its fat, about 10 minutes. Transfer with a slotted spoon to a separate dish.

2. Add the onion to the remaining bacon fat in the pan, season with salt, and cook for 5 minutes, until slightly softened.

3. Add the dates and kale to the pan and season lightly with salt and pepper. Use a wooden spoon to break up the dates.

4. Pour in the chicken broth and vinegar and cook for about 10 minutes, until the kale is soft and the dates are broken down.

5. Return the bacon to the pan and stir to mix before serving.

PAN-ROASTED BRUSSELS SPROUTS

I love the crispy edges of these Brussels sprouts. They need very little seasoning to make them a delicious side dish, but if you're feeling fancy, add some bacon and dates, as in the preceding stewed kale recipe. Or, shower with finely chopped roasted hazelnuts just before serving.

SERVES: 2 to 4   PREP TIME: 10 minutes   COOK TIME: 15 to 20 minutes

2 tablespoons coconut oil

1 pound Brussels sprouts, halved vertically, outer leaves and tough ends of stems removed

sea salt to taste

freshly ground pepper to taste

juice of ½ lemon

1. Preheat the oven to 425°F.

2. Heat the cast iron skillet over medium-high heat until hot, about 2 minutes. Melt the coconut oil and tilt the pan to coat it.

3. Add the Brussels sprouts to the pan, cut-side down. Cook without disturbing for 5 minutes until gently browned. Flip the sprouts so that the cut sides are facing up, season with salt and pepper, and transfer the pan to the oven.

4. Roast for 10 to 15 minutes, until they are tender throughout and crisp on the edges. Shower with lemon juice before serving.

ROASTED KABOCHA SQUASH

I'm in love with roasted kabocha squash. It is amazing when each slice is caramelized on one side, tender throughout, and ensconced in the chewy edible peel. Vegetarian chef Amanda Cohen coined the phrase "dirt candy," and it's a fitting description for this vegetable.

SERVES: 2 to 4   PREP TIME: 5 minutes   COOK TIME: 25 minutes

1 kabocha squash, cut into 1-inch-thick slices

2 tablespoons coconut oil

sea salt to taste

freshly ground pepper to taste

1. Preheat the oven to 425°F.

2. Heat the cast iron skillet over medium-high heat until hot, about 2 minutes.

3. Place the squash in a large bowl and drizzle with the coconut oil, tossing to coat thoroughly.

4. Arrange the squash in the pan so that each piece touches the surface of the pan. Season with salt and pepper. Cook on the stove for 5 minutes then transfer to the oven to finish cooking for 20 minutes, or until tender throughout.

HOW TO CUT A KABOCHA SQUASH: Using a sharp chef's knife, cut the unpeeled squash in half vertically, through the stem. Remove the inner seeds and strings and discard. Lay each half cut-side down, and cut 1-inch-thick slices. Each will resemble the letter "c".

CAPONATA

This eggplant-based dish resembles ratatouille at first glance, but it has a decidedly different texture and a sweet and sour flavor. It's delicious with cold grilled chicken and a simple mixed green salad.

SERVES: 2 to 4   PREP TIME: 10 minutes, plus 30 minutes inactive time   COOK TIME: 20 to 25 minutes

1 large eggplant, cut into ¾-inch cubes

3 to 4 tablespoons extra-virgin olive oil, divided

1 small red onion, thinly sliced

1 celery stalk, finely diced

1 tablespoon capers, rinsed and drained

1 tablespoon minced green olives

1 tablespoon tomato paste

1 tablespoon maple syrup

1 tablespoon red wine vinegar

sea salt to taste

freshly ground pepper to taste

1. Season the eggplant liberally with salt and place in a colander in the sink or over a bowl to drain for 30 minutes. Rinse thoroughly and then squeeze as much moisture as you can from the eggplant.

2. Heat the cast iron skillet over medium heat until hot, about 2 minutes. Add 3 tablespoons of the olive oil and tilt to coat the bottom of the pan. Add the eggplant and cook until browned on all sides, about 10 minutes. Use a slotted spoon to transfer the eggplant to a separate dish.

3. Add the remaining tablespoon of oil to the skillet if none remains from cooking the eggplant. Cook the onion and celery until somewhat soft, 5 to 7 minutes. Add the capers and green olives and cook for another 2 to 3 minutes. Add the tomato paste, maple syrup, and red wine vinegar and cook until beginning to caramelize, another 2 to 3 minutes.

4. Return the eggplant to the pan and season with salt and pepper.

SAUTÉED MUSHROOMS

These mushrooms are bursting with umami flavor and offer the perfect accompaniment to a simple seared steak or chicken breast.

SERVES: 4   PREP TIME: 5 minutes   COOK TIME: 15 minutes

4 to 6 tablespoons ghee or coconut oil, divided

8 ounces (about 2 cups) whole cremini mushrooms, halved

1 teaspoon fresh thyme leaves

1 shallot, minced

2 tablespoons dry sherry

sea salt to taste

freshly ground pepper to taste

1. Heat the cast iron skillet over medium-high heat until hot, about 2 minutes.

2. Melt 2 tablespoons of the ghee or oil in the skillet and tilt to coat the pan. Add enough mushrooms to barely cover the skillet, without crowding them. Cook on the cut side until browned, 1 to 2 minutes.

3. Push the cooked mushrooms to the side and add more ghee and another batch of mushrooms to the pan, cooking in the same manner. Proceed with the remaining ghee and mushrooms until all are cooked. You may not need to use all of the ghee.

4. Add the thyme and shallot to the pan and cook for another 2 minutes.

5. Deglaze the pan with the sherry and season to taste with salt and pepper. Serve warm.

FRIED PLANTAINS AND BACON

This is the ultimate Paleo athlete side dish—replete with complex carbo-hydrates and satisfying fats.

SERVES: 2   PREP TIME: 5 minutes   COOK TIME: 15 to 20 minutes

4 slices applewood-smoked bacon, cut into lardons

2 barely ripe plantains, peeled and cut into ½-inch-thick slices

sea salt to taste

freshly ground pepper to taste

1. Cook the bacon pieces in the cast iron skillet over medium-low heat until the bacon renders most of its fat, about 10 minutes. Transfer the bacon pieces with a slotted spoon to a separate dish.

2. Increase the heat to medium-high. Fry the plantain slices in the bacon fat for about 3 minutes on each side, until well browned. Return the bacon to the pan, season with salt and pepper, and give everything a good toss.

VARIATION: For a mashed potato consistency, transfer the plantains and bacon to a mortar and pestle and mash until thick and soft.

GINGERY BABY BOK CHOY

This tangy Asian side dish goes well with pan-seared seafood such as scallops or salmon. Cook the bok choy first. The fish cooks in just a few minutes thereafter.

SERVES: 2 to 4   PREP TIME: 5 minutes   COOK TIME: 15 minutes

1 tablespoon sesame oil

8 (6-inch-long) baby bok choy, halved lengthwise

2 tablespoons coconut aminos or gluten-free soy sauce

1 teaspoon maple syrup

1 teaspoon minced ginger

1 teaspoon minced garlic

pinch red chili flakes

juice of 1 lime

1. Heat the cast iron skillet over medium-high heat until very hot, about 5 minutes. Melt the sesame oil in the skillet.

2. Place the bok choy cut-side down into the skillet, alternating the direction of each piece so that there is room for all of them. Try to get the root end toward the hottest part of the pan, which is generally the center.

3. Cook the bok choy until browned, about 5 to 7 minutes. Flip the vegetables over and cook for 2 to 3 minutes.

4. In a small bowl, whisk together the coconut aminos or soy sauce, maple syrup, ginger, garlic, red chili flakes, and lime juice. Pour this over the bok choy and simmer for another 5 minutes, until the stems are easily sliced with a butter knife and the greens are tender.

CHAPTER FIVE

Vegetarian

CARAMELIZED GARLIC FRITTATA

Adapted from a Yotam Ottolenghi recipe, this frittata is brimming with flavor but forgoes the cheese and puff pastry present in the original. Blanching the garlic first softens their flavor, so don't skip this step!

SERVES: 2 to 4   PREP TIME: 10 minutes   COOK TIME: 35 minutes

3 heads garlic, cloves separated and peeled

1 tablespoon olive oil

2 tablespoons balsamic vinegar

1 tablespoon maple syrup

1 cup vegetable broth or water

1 small sprig fresh rosemary, needles minced

½ teaspoon minced thyme leaves

8 eggs

½ teaspoon sea salt

freshly ground pepper to taste

1. Preheat the oven to 350°F.

2. Bring a small pot of water to a simmer. Add the peeled garlic cloves and cook for 3 minutes. Drain thoroughly.

3. Heat the olive oil in the cast iron skillet over medium heat. Add the garlic and sauté for 2 minutes.

4. Add the balsamic vinegar, maple syrup, broth or water, rosemary, and thyme. Simmer uncovered for 10 to 15 minutes, or until most of the liquid has evaporated.

5. Whisk the eggs in a large pitcher and season with the salt and several grinds of black pepper. Pour the eggs into the skillet and cook for about 5 minutes.

6. Place the skillet into the oven and continue cooking until the top is set, about 10 minutes. Allow to cool for 5 minutes before slicing and serving.

EGGPLANT INVOLTINI

The nut-based "ricotta" cheese in this decadent vegan dinner takes a bit of advanced preparation, but it's definitely worth the effort. And it takes less active time to make than cow's milk ricotta!

SERVES: 2 to 4   PREP TIME: 20 minutes, plus 8 hours inactive time   COOK TIME: 45 minutes

2 cups blanched almonds

1 cup water

¼ teaspoon sea salt, plus more for seasoning

2 eggplants, thinly sliced lengthwise

¼ cup olive oil, divided

¼ cup toasted pine nuts

¼ cup raisins, roughly chopped

¼ cup minced parsley

2 tablespoons minced fresh mint

2 garlic cloves, minced

1 teaspoon finely grated lemon zest

1 cup canned pureed tomatoes

½ cup shredded fresh basil

freshly ground pepper to taste

1. Soak the almonds overnight in fresh water. Rinse thoroughly and add to a blender with the water and salt. Blend until thick and mostly smooth.

2. Transfer the mixture to a nut milk bag and hang from a sink handle or cabinet knob over a bowl to drain for 1 hour. Refrigerate until ready to use.

3. Meanwhile, season the eggplant slices generously with salt and set in a colander to release moisture for 30 minutes. Rinse under cool water and wring out excess moisture.

4. Heat a tablespoon of the olive oil in the cast iron skillet over medium heat. Cook the eggplant slices for about 2 to 3 minutes on each side, until gently browned. Transfer to a separate platter to cool, and cook the remaining eggplant slices in batches, adding additional olive oil as needed.

5. In a small bowl, combine the almond "cheese" with the pine nuts, raisins, parsley, mint, garlic, and lemon zest. Season with salt and pepper.

6. Preheat the oven to 375°F.

7. Take a cooled eggplant slice and fill it with a small scoop of the filling. Roll the eggplant around the filling and place seam-side down in the cast iron skillet. Repeat until all of the eggplant slices and filling are used up. Top the involtini with the tomato puree.

8. Transfer the skillet to the oven and bake for 25 to 30 minutes. Shower with the fresh basil. Allow to rest for 10 minutes before serving.

INGREDIENT TIP: You can also check out your specialty health food store for the increasing selection of nut-based cheeses available.

CAULIFLOWER FRIED RICE

There's something comforting about cuddling up to a big bowl of fried rice and watching reruns. Here's a Paleo version that will complete your Seinfeld fix without the carb hangover.

SERVES: 2 to 4   PREP TIME: 5 minutes   COOK TIME: 15 to 17 minutes

4 slices pancetta or bacon, cut into lardons

2 eggs, whisked

1 tablespoon toasted sesame oil (optional)

1 tablespoon minced ginger

1 tablespoon minced garlic

⅛ teaspoon red chili flakes

1 head cauliflower, riced

1 cup frozen peas, defrosted

2 tablespoons coconut aminos or gluten-free soy sauce

2 green onions, thinly sliced on a bias

sea salt to taste

freshly ground pepper to taste

1. Cook the pancetta over medium-low heat until it has rendered most of its fat and is almost crispy, about 10 minutes. Use a slotted spoon to transfer it to a separate dish.

2. Pour the eggs into the pan and cook without disturbing, as if making an omelet, until nearly set, about 2 minutes. Use a spatula to carefully flip the eggs and fry on the other side for 30 seconds. Transfer the cooked eggs to a cutting board, allow to cool, and slice into thin ribbons.

3. Add the toasted sesame oil to the pan, if using, and cook the ginger, garlic, and red chili flakes until fragrant, 1 to 2 minutes.

4. Increase the heat to medium. Add the cauliflower and peas to the pan, and sauté for 2 minutes, until barely softened.

5. Stir in the coconut aminos or soy sauce, green onions, cooked pancetta, and cooked eggs. Season to taste with salt and pepper, and serve.

COOKING TIP: To "rice" the cauliflower, pulse it in a food processor fitted with the standard blade until it forms small granules that resemble couscous. If you do not have a food processor, you can grate it using a box grater.

SHAKSHUKA

The key to a good shakshuka is vine-ripe tomatoes and a generous dose of spices. If it's not tomato season and you're still craving this fiery main dish, use canned whole plum tomatoes.

SERVES: 2 to 4 PREP TIME: 10 minutes COOK TIME: 35 minutes

½ teaspoon cumin seed

¼ teaspoon caraway seed

2 tablespoons olive oil

1 yellow onion, halved and thinly sliced

1 green bell pepper, cored, seeded, and thinly sliced

1 red bell pepper, cored, seeded, and thinly sliced

½ serrano pepper, minced

4 cloves garlic, minced

2 tablespoons tomato paste

¼ teaspoon smoked paprika

6 cups diced fresh tomatoes

1 bay leaf

1 teaspoon sea salt

6 to 8 eggs

1. Toast the cumin and caraway seed in a dry cast-iron skillet over medium heat until fragrant, about 2 minutes. Transfer the spices to a mortar and coarsely grind.

2. Heat the olive oil in the same skillet over medium heat. Cook the onion, green and red peppers, and serrano for about 5 minutes, until slightly softened. Add the garlic and cook for another minute.

3. Stir in the tomato paste and smoked paprika, and cook for another minute.

4. Add the tomatoes, bay leaf, cumin, and caraway. Season with salt. Simmer uncovered for 20 minutes.

5. Make several indentations in the stew and crack an egg into each one. Continue cooking for another 5 to 7 minutes, or until the egg whites are set.

TORTILLA ESPAÑOLA

Tortilla is enjoyed in Spain as a tapa and the cast iron skillet is the perfect vessel for preparing it because it is naturally nonstick but produces a beautiful brown crust. I like to serve this dish with several vegetable side dishes for dinner.

SERVES: 2 to 4   PREP TIME: 5 minutes   COOK TIME: 20 minutes

2 tablespoons coconut oil

2 potatoes, thinly sliced

½ green bell pepper, cored and thinly sliced

½ yellow onion, thinly sliced

½ teaspoon sea salt

¼ cup dry white wine

8 eggs, whisked

1. Preheat the oven to 350°F.

2. Heat the coconut oil in the cast iron skillet over medium heat. Cook the potatoes, bell pepper, and onion until gently browned and nearly soft, then add the salt.

3. Add the white wine and continue cooking until nearly all of the liquid has cooked down.

4. Pour in the eggs. Continue cooking for 5 minutes. Transfer the pan to the oven for 10 minutes, or until set.

5. Slice into wedges to serve.

COOKING TIP: For a more authentic method, cook the tortilla only over the stove top. After pouring in the eggs, cook until set and then remove it from the pan, flip, and return to the pan carefully. Continue cooking on the stove top for another 2 to 3 minutes.

COCONUT-CRUSTED PLANTAIN TACOS

This was one of the first recipes I tested for this book and it is so delicious I wanted to hang up my apron and call it a day. The crunchiness of the coconut offset by the tangy avocado crema is just divine! Serve as an appetizer or with cauliflower rice as a complete meal.

SERVES: 2 to 4   PREP TIME: 10 minutes   COOK TIME: 10 minutes

1 avocado, diced

juice of 2 limes

2 tablespoons olive oil

sea salt to taste

2 tablespoons coconut oil

2 ripe plantains, sliced in half lengthwise and again across so that each fruit yields 4 equal pieces

1 egg white, whisked

½ cup unsweetened shredded coconut

8 lettuce leaves

¼ cup minced red onion

1. Combine the avocado, lime juice, and olive oil in a blender and puree until smooth. Season with salt. Set aside.

2. Heat the coconut oil in the cast iron skillet over medium heat until hot.

3. Dip each piece of plantain in the whisked egg white and then dredge in the shredded coconut. Place the plantain pieces into the skillet and sear for about 1 to 2 minutes on each side, until browned on all sides.

4. Place one fried plantain slice into each lettuce leaf and top with a drizzle of the avocado puree and a pinch of minced onion. Serve immediately.

VARIATION: Transform the fried plantains into a scrumptious dessert. Add 1 teaspoon of ground cinnamon to the whisked egg white. Dip the plantain slices into it and then dredge in the shredded coconut and proceed as directed. Serve with Paleo coconut ice cream.

BROCCOLI MUSHROOM CASSEROLE

This is Paleo, vegetarian comfort food at its finest. Pair it with a glass of hard cider or bone dry white wine.

SERVES: 2 to 4   PREP TIME: 10 minutes   COOK TIME: 40 minutes

3 tablespoons ghee or extra-virgin olive oil, divided

2 cups sliced cremini mushrooms

1 yellow onion, diced

2 cloves garlic, minced

pinch red chili flakes

1 teaspoon fresh thyme leaves

4 cups steamed fresh broccoli (frozen and defrosted is okay)

1 cup full-fat coconut milk

2 eggs

½ teaspoon sea salt

1. Preheat the oven to 400°F.

2. Heat the cast iron skillet over medium-high heat until hot, about 2 minutes. Add 1 tablespoon of the olive oil and tilt to coat the bottom of the pan. Cook the mushrooms in three batches, adding another table-spoon of oil as needed, until they are well browned, making sure not to crowd the pan. This should take about 2 to 3 minutes per batch. Push the cooked mushrooms to the sides of the pan.

3. Add the onion, garlic, red chili flakes, and thyme to the pan. Cook until beginning to soften, about 5 minutes.

4. Add the broccoli and stir to mix with the other ingredients. Cook just until the broccoli is heated through.

5. In a separate container, whisk the coconut milk, eggs, and sea salt together. Pour this over the vegetable mixture. Transfer the pan to the oven and bake for 20 minutes, or until golden brown on the top and bubbling.

FRIED PLANTAIN AND COLLARD BOWLS

I made this recipe for lunch one afternoon and was undone by how easy and delicious it was, especially when drizzled with the Vegan Chipotle Aioli. For a simple non-vegan version, whip up ½ cup of Paleo-friendly mayonnaise with 1 tablespoon of adobo sauce.

SERVES: 2   PREP TIME: 5 minutes   COOK TIME: 10 minutes

3 tablespoons coconut oil, divided

2 barely-ripe plantains, sliced in ½-inch-thick slices

1 bunch collard greens, ribs removed, thinly sliced in ribbons

1 teaspoon minced garlic

½ cup Vegan Chipotle Aioli (recipe follows)

sea salt to taste

1. Preheat the cast iron skillet over medium-high heat. Add 2 tablespoons of the coconut oil, tilting to coat the pan.

2. Fry the plantain slices until browned, about 3 minutes on each side. Transfer the plantains to individual serving dishes. Season with salt.

3. Add the remaining tablespoon of coconut oil to the pan, and then add the collard greens and garlic. Sauté until the greens are bright and barely wilted, about 2 minutes. Season with salt. Divide them between the serving bowls.

4. Drizzle the bowls with Vegan Chipotle Aioli.

VEGAN CHIPOTLE AIOLI

YIELD: ¾ cup   PREP TIME: 5 minutes, plus 4 hours inactive time

½ cup cashews

¼ cup of fresh water

1 clove garlic

1 teaspoon lime juice

1 chipotle in adobo

1 tablespoon adobo sauce

1 tablespoon extra-virgin olive oil

sea salt

1. Soak the cashews in water for at least 4 hours or overnight. Rinse thoroughly and drain.

2. Place the soaked cashews in a blender with the water, garlic, lime juice, chipotle, adobo sauce, and extra-virgin olive oil. Blend until smooth, adding more water as needed. Season to taste with salt.

PREPARATION TIP: To slice the collard greens, remove the ribs and roll the leaves into a tight cylinder lengthwise. Use a chef's knife to cut the greens in ⅛-inch-thick slices off the end, which will produce thin ribbons.

ROASTED BUTTERNUT SQUASH CHILI

What it lacks in traditional chili ingredients—beans and meat—this chili makes up for in flavor. It strikes the perfect balance between smoky, sweet, and spicy.

SERVES: 2 to 4   PREP TIME: 10 minutes   COOK TIME: 35 minutes

1 butternut squash (about 4 cups total), peeled, seeded, and cut into 1-inch cubes

1 yellow onion, thinly sliced

1 green bell pepper, cored and thinly sliced

2 tablespoons coconut oil

2 garlic cloves, minced

2 roasted red bell peppers, diced

1 (15-ounce) can fire-roasted diced tomatoes

2 teaspoons smoked paprika

1 teaspoon ground cumin

⅛ teaspoon cayenne pepper

1 avocado, pitted and sliced, for serving

sea salt to taste

freshly ground pepper to taste

1. Preheat the oven to 375°F.

2. Combine the butternut squash, onion, and bell pepper in the cast iron skillet. Drizzle with the coconut oil and toss gently to coat. Season with salt. Roast uncovered for 30 minutes.

3. Carefully remove the pan to the stove top and add the garlic, red bell peppers, tomatoes, paprika, cumin, and cayenne. Bring to a simmer over medium-low heat. Season to taste with salt and pepper. Scoop into individual serving bowls and top with a few slices of avocado.

HOW TO CUT A BUTTERNUT SQUASH: Use a vegetable peeler to remove the thick outer skin. Cut the squash in half lengthwise. Use a spoon to scoop out the seeds and strings. Cut away the stem end and cut the remaining flesh into 1-inch cubes, or as directed.

SIZZLING PORTOBELLO FAJITAS

Mushrooms make a healthy and delicious (not to mention inexpensive) stand-in for steak in these simple fajitas. Use cabbage or lettuce leaves or purchase premade Paleo-friendly wraps. They're especially awesome with the Vegan Chipotle Aioli (page 62).

SERVES: 2   PREP TIME: 5 minutes   COOK TIME: 15 to 20 minutes

2 tablespoons coconut oil

1 green bell pepper, cored and thinly sliced

1 red or yellow bell pepper, cored and thinly sliced

1 yellow onion, halved and thinly sliced

2 portobello mushrooms, stems removed, thinly sliced

½ teaspoon ground coriander

1 teaspoon ground cumin

1 teaspoon chipotle chili powder

sea salt to taste

freshly ground pepper to taste

8 butter lettuce leaves, for serving

1 avocado, pitted and thinly sliced

¼ cup roughly chopped cilantro

1. Heat the cast iron skillet over medium-high heat until hot, about 2 minutes. Add the coconut oil to the pan and tilt to coat. Add the bell peppers and onion, and sauté for 8 to 10 minutes, until the onion is golden throughout and the edges begin to brown.

2. Push the onions and peppers to the sides of the pan and add the portobello slices to the center. Cook for 5 to 7 minutes, until browned on each side.

3. Add the coriander, cumin, and chili powder to the vegetables, and season with salt and black pepper.

4. To serve, scoop some of the mushrooms, onion, and peppers into a lettuce leaf and top with a slice of avocado and a pinch of cilantro.

MINT AND PEA FRITTERS

Peas are a gray area in Paleo because they're technically a legume. However, green peas are not the same as dry beans and have been bred to be enjoyed and easily digested when plucked fresh off the vine. They're delicious with a dairy-free Cucumber Mint Raita (recipe follows).

SERVES: 2 (about 8 fritters)   PREP TIME: 5 minutes   COOK TIME: 10 minutes

¼ cup coconut flour

¼ teaspoon sea salt

¼ teaspoon baking powder

⅓ cup almond milk or light coconut milk

2 eggs

1 cup green peas, frozen and defrosted

1 green onion, white and green parts thinly sliced

2 tablespoons minced fresh mint

2 tablespoons coconut oil

1 cup Cucumber Mint Raita

1. Combine the coconut flour, sea salt, and baking powder in a small mixing bowl.

2. Pour in the almond milk and eggs. Whisk to combine.

3. Fold in the peas, green onion, and mint. Allow the mixture to rest and thicken for about 2 minutes while you heat the pan over a medium heat.

4. Melt 1 tablespoon of the coconut oil and tilt to coat the bottom of the pan.

5. Scoop the fritter batter into the pan, using a ¼ cup measuring cup. Cook for about 3 minutes, until gently browned. Flip and cook on the other side for 2 to 3 minutes. Transfer to a cooling rack and proceed with the remaining batter. Serve with the Cucumber Mint Raita. Use extra oil to fry remaining fritters.

CUCUMBER MINT RAITA

YIELD: 1 cup   PREP TIME: 5 minutes

6 ounces coconut or almond milk yogurt

½ cup finely diced cucumber

1 tablespoon minced fresh mint

1 tablespoon minced cilantro

1 tablespoon minced shallot

sea salt

freshly ground pepper

Combine the yogurt, cucumber, mint, cilantro, and shallot. Mix well. Season to taste with salt and pepper.

SCALLION CAULIFLOWER PANCAKE

This vegetarian appetizer or entrée is a cross between a fritter and a hash brown. It is delicious with a simple Paleo Lemon Garlic Aioli (recipe follows).

SERVES: 2 to 4   PREP TIME: 10 minutes, plus 30 minutes inactive time   COOK TIME: 15 minutes

1 head cauliflower, grated, about 4 cups total

¾ teaspoon sea salt, divided

4 scallions, white and green parts, thinly sliced on a bias

1 egg, whisked

1 clove garlic, minced

freshly ground pepper to taste

¼ cup coconut flour

½ teaspoon baking powder

2 tablespoons coconut oil

1. Place the grated cauliflower in a colander and sprinkle with half a teaspoon of the sea salt. Allow to sit for 30 minutes over the sink. Rinse the cauliflower and squeeze out excess moisture.

2. Combine the cauliflower with the remaining ¼ teaspoon sea salt, scallions, egg, and garlic. Season with pepper.

3. Sift the coconut flour and baking powder together and then add to the cauliflower mixture. Mix thoroughly. Allow the mixture to rest while you heat the pan.

4. Heat the cast iron skillet over medium-high heat until hot, about 2 minutes. Add 1 tablespoon of the coconut oil and tilt to coat the bottom of the pan. Scoop ¼-cup portions of the cauliflower mixture into the pan and press into a cake with a metal spatula. Cook on each side for 4 to 5 minutes, until browned. Flip and cook on the opposite side for another 4 to 5 minutes. Top with the Lemon Garlic Aioli. Use extra oil to fry remaining pancakes.

LEMON GARLIC AIOLI

YIELD: ¾ cup   PREP TIME: 5 minutes

1 teaspoon lemon zest

1 teaspoon lemon juice

¼ teaspoon sea salt

1 clove garlic, minced

1 egg yolk

¾ cup macadamia or avocado oil

1. Whisk together the lemon zest, lemon juice, salt, garlic, and egg yolk.

2. Slowly drizzle in the oil a few drops at a time, whisking constantly to emulsify. Refrigerate until ready to serve.

CHAPTER SIX

Fish and Seafood

PAN-SEARED SALMON OVER MIXED GREENS

Growing up in the Pacific Northwest instilled in me a lasting appreciation for perfectly cooked salmon. The cast iron skillet does a beautiful job of creating a crisp sear on the outside while leaving the inner flesh moist and a brilliant coral color.

SERVES: 2   PREP TIME: 10 minutes   COOK TIME: 5 minutes

3 tablespoons toasted sesame oil, divided

juice of 1 lime

1 teaspoon minced ginger

½ teaspoon minced garlic

2 cups spring mix

½ cup hand-torn fresh basil

½ cup roughly chopped fresh cilantro

1 cup diced cucumber, unpeeled if organic

2 salmon filets, about 6 ounces each

sea salt to taste

freshly ground pepper to taste

1. Begin by making the salad dressing. Combine 2 tablespoons of the sesame oil with the lime juice, ginger, and garlic. Season with salt and pepper.

2. In a large salad bowl, combine the spring mix, basil, cilantro, and cucumber. Set aside.

3. Heat the cast iron skillet over medium heat until hot, about 2 minutes.

4. Coat the salmon filets with the remaining tablespoon of sesame oil and season with salt and pepper. Sear for about 2 minutes on each side for medium-rare. The inside will be deep pink when you remove them from the pan but will continue cooking for a minute or two thereafter.

5. Toss the salad with the dressing and divide between serving plates. Top the salads with the seared salmon.

CHILEAN SEA BASS WITH GRAPE TOMATOES

Chilean sea bass is the fish I buy when I really want an impressive seafood dinner, especially when I'm cooking for someone who is on the fence about fish. It has a mild flavor and a texture similar to that of sea scallops, with a price tag to match.

SERVES: 2   PREP TIME: 5 minutes   COOK TIME: 5 to 7 minutes

2 tablespoons extra-virgin olive oil

2 Chilean sea bass filets, about 4 to 6 ounces each

1 pint grape tomatoes, halved

4 cloves garlic, thinly sliced

¼ cup roughly chopped fresh parsley

2 tablespoons finely chopped toasted pine nuts

1 lemon, cut into wedges

sea salt to taste

freshly ground pepper to taste

1. Heat the cast iron skillet over medium-high heat until hot, about 2 minutes.

2. Add the olive oil to the skillet and tilt to coat the surface of the pan. Season the fish generously with salt and pepper. Sear for 3 to 4 minutes, until you get a good brown crust, basting regularly with olive oil from the pan. Flip and cook on the other side until the fish flakes easily with a fork and is opaque throughout, about 2 to 3 additional minutes.

3. Remove the fish to a serving platter. Add the tomatoes, garlic, and parsley to the pan, and season with salt and pepper. Give everything a good toss and cook for about 2 minutes, until heated through and fragrant. Top the fish with the tomato mixture and sprinkle with the toasted pine nuts. Serve the lemon wedges on the side.

INGREDIENT TIP: Look for Chilean sea bass sold with the Marine Stewardship Council's seal of approval for the best quality fish with the least likelihood of environmental concerns and mercury contamination.

SOLE MEUNIÈRE

The first time I made this dish, I lived in England and bought Dover sole from a merchant on the rocky coast of the North Sea. His boats were still wet with seawater and he wrapped the fish in the newspapers filled with the latest gossip about the royal family. Although this dish is traditionally served with the fish cooked whole and fileted at the table, I prefer not to futz with removing bones and skin when what I really want is to eat!

SERVES: 2   PREP TIME: 5 minutes   COOK TIME: 5 to 10 minutes

2 (6-ounce) sole filets

sea salt to taste

freshly ground pepper to taste

2 tablespoons coconut flour

2 tablespoons coconut oil or ghee

juice of 1 lemon

1 tablespoon capers, rinsed and drained (optional)

¼ cup minced fresh parsley

1. Season the sole filets liberally with salt and pepper, and sprinkle with the coconut flour to coat lightly.

2. Heat the cast iron skillet over medium heat until very hot, about 4 minutes.

3. Add the coconut oil or ghee to the pan and swirl to coat. Sear the fish for 2 minutes, until golden brown and crisp. Flip the fish and add the lemon juice and capers, if using, to the pan. Cook for another minute and serve garnished with the parsley.

INGREDIENT TIP: In the United States, Pacific sole is a good alternative to Dover sole. However, avoid the overfished Atlantic sole.

CLASSIC SAUCE VARIATION: Traditional recipes for Sole Meunière call for butter in absolutely decadent amounts. If you tolerate dairy, whip up this simple pan sauce. Transfer the cooked fish to a serving platter and remove the pan from the heat. Whisk 4 tablespoons of cold butter into the pan about a teaspoon at a time until a thick sauce forms. Return the fish to the pan or drizzle the sauce over the cooked fish on the serving platter.

CAJUN BLACKENED HALIBUT

This spicy rub blackens as it cooks and makes a stunning contrast to the milky white fish flesh. Halibut has a nicer flavor and texture than cod, but it is more expensive so use whatever suits your taste and budget. Serve with simple steamed broccolini and sweet potatoes.

SERVES: 4   PREP TIME: 10 minutes   COOK TIME: 8 to 10 minutes

1 tablespoon minced fresh thyme leaves

1 tablespoon minced fresh oregano

1 tablespoon minced fresh parsley

1 teaspoon minced garlic

2 teaspoons smoked paprika

¼ teaspoon cayenne pepper

½ teaspoon sea salt

¼ teaspoon freshly ground black pepper

1 tablespoon extra-virgin olive oil

1 lemon cut into wedges, plus 1 tablespoon lemon juice

4 (6-ounce) halibut filets

1. Combine the thyme, oregano, parsley, garlic, paprika, cayenne pepper, sea salt, and black pepper with a mortar and pestle. Drizzle in the olive oil and lemon juice. Bash until the mixture forms a thick paste. Spread the mixture onto the fish filets.

2. Heat the cast iron skillet over medium heat until hot, about 2 minutes.

3. Sear the fish for about 3 to 4 minutes on each side. Serve with lemon wedges.

SESAME-CRUSTED TUNA

Make sure to purchase flash-frozen tuna instead of "fresh" tuna from the fish counter. Unless you're shopping at a top-notch fish market, the latter has been thawing for who knows how long and is unsuitable for the rare cooking temperature that is ideal for tuna. I like to serve this over a bed of mixed greens and herbs with a simple soy-ginger vinaigrette.

SERVES: 2   PREP TIME: 5 minutes   COOK TIME: 5 minutes

2 (6-ounce) ahi tuna steaks

1 tablespoon toasted sesame oil

sea salt to taste

freshly ground pepper to taste

½ cup sesame seeds

1. Heat the cast iron skillet over medium heat until hot, about 2 minutes.

2. Pat the tuna steaks dry with a paper towel. Coat with the sesame oil and then season on all sides with salt and pepper.

3. Spread the sesame seeds on a small plate and place the tuna into the seeds to coat on all sides.

4. Place the tuna into the cast iron skillet and cook for 1 to 2 minutes on each side, for rare. The inside should be deep pink but warm. Serve immediately.

GARLIC AND LEMON SEARED PRAWNS

The cast iron skillet provides the high heat to get a good sear on these prawns. Start to finish, the recipe is on the table in less than 10 minutes, making it a great weeknight supper or summertime dinner. Serve them with a simple salad of mixed greens and a crisp glass of Sauvignon Blanc.

SERVES: 2   PREP TIME: 5 minutes   COOK TIME: 5 minutes

1 pound colossal or extra-jumbo shrimp (about 20 shrimp/pound)

1 tablespoon coconut oil, melted

¼ teaspoon sea salt

1 teaspoon minced garlic

pinch red chili flakes

zest and juice of 1 lemon

1. Peel the shrimp, leaving the tails on. Combine them with the coconut oil, sea salt, garlic, red chili flakes, and lemon zest. Toss to coat thoroughly. This step may be done several hours in advance; store the shrimp in a nonreactive dish in the refrigerator.

2. Heat the cast iron skillet over medium-high heat until hot, about 2 minutes.

3. Add the shrimp to the cast iron skillet and sear for 1 to 2 minutes on each side, turning over once with tongs, until cooked through and opaque but not curled tightly (this indicates overcooking).

4. Shower with the fresh lemon juice and serve immediately.

PROSCIUTTO-WRAPPED SCALLOPS AND SAUTÉED COLLARDS

Sweet, savory, and oh so delicious, these prosciutto-wrapped scallops are a cinch to throw together. The scallops and collard greens cook in an instant, so have all of the ingredients prepared before you get started.

SERVES: 2   PREP TIME: 10 minutes   COOK TIME: 5 minutes

8 to 12 jumbo sea scallops, about 1 pound

4 to 6 slices prosciutto, halved lengthwise

1 tablespoon coconut oil

1 bunch collard greens, thinly sliced in ribbons

1 green apple, peeled, cored, and finely diced

1 shallot, minced

sea salt to taste

freshly ground pepper to taste

1. Heat the cast iron skillet over medium-high heat until hot, about 2 minutes.

2. Meanwhile, pat the scallops dry with a paper towel. Wrap one slice of prosciutto around each scallop, securing with a toothpick. Season both sides with salt and pepper.

3. Add the coconut oil to the pan and tilt to coat the bottom of the pan. When the oil is hot, place the scallops into the pan and cook for 1 to 2 minutes on each side, until thoroughly browned. Transfer the scallops to a separate dish.

4. Add the collard greens, apple, and shallot to the pan, and sauté for about 2 minutes, until the collards are bright green. Season with salt and pepper.

5. Divide the greens between serving plates and top with the scallops.

BOK CHOY AND SCALLOP STIR-FRY

Cooking goes fast with this savory stir-fry, so have all of the ingredients ready before you begin.

SERVES: 2 to 4   PREP TIME: 10 minutes   COOK TIME: 15 minutes

1 tablespoon toasted sesame oil

8 baby bok choy, roughly chopped

1 red bell pepper, cored and sliced lengthwise

1 tablespoon minced garlic

1 tablespoon minced ginger

⅛ teaspoon red chili flakes

16 ounces bay scallops

2 tablespoons chicken broth

2 tablespoons gluten-free soy sauce or coconut aminos

1 teaspoon rice wine vinegar

1 teaspoon tapioca starch

2 green onions, thinly sliced on a bias

1 tablespoon toasted sesame seed

1. Heat the sesame oil in the cast iron skillet over medium-high heat. When it is hot, add the bok choy and red bell pepper. Sauté for 2 to 3 minutes.

2. Add the garlic, ginger, and red chili flakes to the pan, and cook for 30 seconds until fragrant.

3. Push the vegetables to the side of the pan and add the scallops. Cook for about 1 to 2 minutes, or until opaque.

4. Whisk together the chicken broth, gluten-free soy sauce, rice wine vinegar, and tapioca starch. Pour this mixture over the stir-fry and cook for another minute, or until it forms a thick glaze.

5. Add the green onions and toasted sesame seeds, and mix before serving.

MUSSELS IN THAI COCONUT BROTH

Shrimp is a more common seafood option at Thai restaurants, but mussels are beautiful, delicious, and replete with minerals and omega-3 fatty acids.

SERVES: 4   PREP TIME: 10 minutes   COOK TIME: 10 to 15 minutes

1 tablespoon coconut oil

1 red onion, halved and sliced

4 cloves garlic, minced

1-inch piece ginger, minced

1-inch piece galangal, minced

1 Thai chili, minced

2 pounds mussels

1 (4-inch) segment lemongrass, halved lengthwise

10 kaffir lime leaves

1 tablespoon fish sauce

1 (15-ounce) can coconut milk

1 tablespoon lime juice

sea salt to taste

freshly ground pepper to taste

½ cup fresh cilantro leaves

1. Heat the coconut oil in the cast iron skillet. Cook the onion, garlic, ginger, galangal, and chili until fragrant and barely softened, about 5 minutes.

2. Add the mussels, lemongrass, and kaffir lime leaves. Toss everything to mix. Add the fish sauce and coconut milk. Cover and simmer until the mussels are all opened, about 5 to 7 minutes. Remove the cooked mussels to a serving dish. Stir in the lime juice and season to taste with salt and pepper.

3. Pour the coconut broth over the mussels and shower with cilantro before serving.

SAUSAGE AND MUSSELS IN RICH TOMATO BROTH

It doesn't get much more decadent than this sausage-studded wine and tomato broth with steamed mussels. Scrub and debeard the mussels just before you begin cooking; they are alive until then.

SERVES: 4   PREP TIME: 15 minutes   COOK TIME: 25 to 30 minutes

2 tablespoons olive oil

2 shallots, halved and thinly sliced

6 cloves garlic, smashed

3 links spicy Italian sausage, casings removed

½ cup dry red wine

½ cup chicken broth

1 tablespoon tomato paste

1 cup whole plum tomatoes, crushed by hand

1 sprig fresh thyme

½ cup hand-torn fresh basil

2 pounds fresh mussels, scrubbed and debearded

sea salt to taste

freshly ground pepper to taste

1. Heat the olive oil in the cast iron skillet over medium heat. Add the shallots and garlic, and cook until somewhat softened, about 5 to 7 minutes.

2. Add the Italian sausage to the pan and cook until browned and cooked through, another 5 to 7 minutes.

3. Add the red wine, chicken broth, tomato paste, tomatoes, and thyme to the pan, and bring to a simmer. Cook for 10 minutes until the liquid is reduced by about half.

4. Add the fresh basil and mussels to the pan, give everything a good toss, cover with a lid or a round pan, and cook until the mussels have steamed open, about 5 minutes.

5. Season with salt and pepper.

PESCETARIAN VERSION: If you follow a pescetarian diet or otherwise prefer to omit the sausage, use 1 tablespoon of crushed fennel seed and ¼ teaspoon of crushed red chili flakes in its place. Increase the amount of mussels to 3 pounds and use fish stock or vegetable broth in place of the chicken broth.

NICARAGUAN RUNDOWN STEW

Native to Nicaragua and Costa Rica, rundown stew is a coconut-based soup that includes a haphazard assembly of whatever fish and meat you have on hand, so don't worry too much if you don't have every ingredient on the list.

SERVES: 4   PREP TIME: 10 minutes   COOK TIME: 25 to 30 minutes

1 tablespoon coconut oil

½ pound boneless pork loin, cut into 1-inch pieces

1 stalk celery, diced

1 yellow onion, diced

1 tablespoon minced garlic

1 (15-ounce) can coconut cream or full-fat coconut milk

32 ounces chicken broth

2 sweet potatoes, peeled and diced, about 2 cups total

1 green plantain, cut into large chunks

1 red bell pepper, cored and thinly sliced

1 jalapeño pepper, seeded and minced

1 teaspoon fresh thyme leaves

1 pound large shrimp, peeled

1 pound sea bass, cut into 2-inch pieces

sea salt to taste

freshly ground pepper to taste

1. Heat the cast iron skillet over medium-high heat until hot, about 2 minutes. Add the coconut oil to the pan and tilt to coat the bottom of the pan.

2. Season the pork liberally with salt and pepper. Sear it on all sides until browned, about 3 to 5 minutes. It will not be cooked through. Transfer the meat to a separate dish.

3. Add the celery, onion, and garlic to the pan, and cook for 2 minutes. Pour in the coconut cream, scraping up the browned bits from the bottom of the pan. Add the chicken broth, sweet potatoes, plantain, bell pepper, jalapeño pepper, and thyme leaves. Bring to a simmer for 10 minutes, until the vegetables are beginning to soften.

4. Add the pork, shrimp, and sea bass and cook until the meat and seafood is cooked through, about 10 more minutes. Season to taste with salt and pepper. Cover and allow to rest for a few minutes to let the flavors combine.

CHAPTER SEVEN

Poultry

MEDITERRANEAN CHICKEN

You can prepare this recipe with minimal effort and mess. It's perfect after a long workday when you want comfort food without the cleanup.

SERVES: 2   PREP TIME: 5 minutes   COOK TIME: 40 minutes

1 tablespoon coconut oil

4 to 6 chicken drumsticks (about 1½ pounds), skin on

sea salt to taste

freshly ground pepper to taste

1 cup rinsed, drained artichoke hearts

1 cup grape tomatoes

6 cloves garlic, smashed

1 teaspoon fresh thyme leaves

2 tablespoons minced fresh parsley

juice of ½ lemon

1. Preheat the oven to 375°F. Heat the cast iron skillet over medium-high heat until hot, about 2 minutes. Melt the coconut oil in the pan.

2. Pat the chicken drumsticks dry with paper towels and season generously with salt and pepper. Sear the chicken on all sides in the skillet until gently browned, about 10 minutes total. Add the artichoke hearts, tomatoes, garlic, and thyme to the pan. Transfer to the oven and roast uncovered for 25 to 30 minutes, until the chicken is cooked through and the tomatoes are very soft.

3. Sprinkle with the fresh parsley and shower the tomatoes and artichoke hearts with lemon juice. Serve directly from the skillet.

HONEY MUSTARD ROSEMARY CHICKEN THIGHS

You can't go wrong with the classic flavors of honey, mustard, and fresh rosemary. Maple syrup is a fine substitution for honey.

SERVES: 2 to 4   PREP TIME: 10 minutes, plus 30 minutes to 8 hours inactive time   COOK TIME: 25 minutes

1 tablespoon honey

1 tablespoon lemon juice

1 tablespoon Dijon mustard

1 tablespoon minced fresh rosemary

3 tablespoons extra-virgin olive oil, divided

½ teaspoon sea salt

¼ teaspoon freshly ground pepper

6 to 8 bone-in, skin-on chicken thighs, about 2 pounds

1 pound carrots, scrubbed and cut into 2-inch segments

1. Mix the honey, lemon juice, mustard, rosemary, 2 tablespoons of olive oil, sea salt, and pepper together in a nonreactive dish. Add the chicken thighs and turn to coat thoroughly in the mixture. Refrigerate for at least 30 minutes, or up to 8 hours.

2. Preheat the oven to 350°F. Heat the cast iron skillet over medium heat until hot, about 2 minutes.

3. Remove the chicken from the honey mustard mixture. Place them skin-side down in the skillet. Sear for 3 to 4 minutes, or until a good brown crust forms.

4. Toss the carrots in the remaining marinade, adding the remaining tablespoon of olive oil.

5. Flip the chicken, add the carrots to the pan, and place into the oven. Roast for 20 to 25 minutes, or until the chicken is cooked through to an internal temperature of 165°F and the juices run clear.

COOKING TIP: To get a better sear on the chicken, pat the thighs dry with paper towels. You will lose some of the flavor from the marinade, but you'll gain a delicious golden crust.

CHICKEN AND SAUSAGE IN RUSTIC TOMATO BASIL SAUCE

The combination of flavors in this rustic, one-pan meal is surprisingly complex for how little effort it requires. Look for Paleo-friendly sausage made with sustainably raised pork without the use of antibiotics and without added sugar and nitrites.

SERVES: 2 to 4   PREP TIME: 10 minutes   COOK TIME: 40 minutes

1 tablespoon coconut oil

6 to 8 bone-in chicken thighs (about 2 pounds total), skin removed

2 spicy Italian sausages, cut into 1-inch pieces

½ red onion, sliced

2 cloves garlic, minced

¼ cup dry red wine

1 (28-ounce) can whole plum tomatoes, drained, hand crushed

1 cup roughly chopped fresh basil leaves

sea salt to taste

freshly ground pepper to taste

1. Preheat the oven to 375°F.

2. Heat the cast iron skillet over medium-high heat until hot, about 2 minutes. Add the coconut oil to the skillet and tilt to coat the bottom of the pan.

3. Pat the chicken dry with a paper towel and season generously with salt and pepper. Place it into the skillet top-side (where the skin used to be) down into the skillet. Sear for 3 to 4 minutes, until the chicken is gently browned. Flip the chicken and add the sausage pieces and onion to the pan. Transfer the skillet to the oven and roast for 15 minutes.

4. Combine the garlic, red wine, tomatoes, and basil. Season with salt and pepper. Pour this mixture over the chicken and sausage and return to the oven to cook for another 15 minutes, until the chicken is cooked through to an internal temperature of 165°F.

COOKING TIP: When it's cooked with liquid, chicken skin tends to lose its crispy texture and become limp and unappetizing.

CAST IRON PALEO

CHICKEN ALLA PUTTANESCA

The first time I tasted puttanesca sauce, I was old enough to work in a restaurant but too youthful to keep from snickering at its literal Italian translation— "spaghetti in the style of a prostitute." You can throw it together in minutes, so the story goes. This version features chicken instead of pasta for a filling Paleo meal.

SERVES: 4   PREP TIME: 10 minutes   COOK TIME: 40 minutes

1 tablespoon coconut oil

4 (1½-pound) chicken breasts

1 tablespoon extra-virgin olive oil

1 red onion, halved and thinly sliced

2 cloves garlic, minced

1 teaspoon anchovy paste

pinch red chili flakes

2 tablespoons capers, rinsed and drained

½ cup pitted kalamata olives

1 (28-ounce) can whole plum tomatoes, drained, hand crushed

1 teaspoon minced fresh oregano

2 tablespoons minced fresh parsley

sea salt to taste

freshly ground pepper to taste

1. Preheat the oven to 325°F.

2. Heat the cast iron skillet over medium-high heat until hot, about 2 minutes. Add the coconut oil to the skillet and tilt to coat the bottom of the pan.

3. Pat the chicken dry with a paper towel and season generously with salt and pepper. Place it into the skillet. Sear for 3 to 4 minutes on each side until the chicken is gently browned. Transfer it to a separate dish. It will not be cooked through.

4. Add the olive oil and onion to the pan. Cook for about 5 minutes, until the onion is somewhat softened. Add the garlic, anchovy paste, and red chili flakes. Cook for 2 minutes. Add the capers and olives and cook for another 2 minutes. Add the tomatoes, oregano, and parsley. Season with salt and pepper. Bring to a simmer.

5. Return the chicken to the pan, nestling it down into the sauce. Transfer the skillet to the oven and roast for 25 minutes, until the chicken is cooked through to an internal temperature of 165°F.

CHICKEN WITH MUSHROOMS, PORT, AND SHALLOTS

This simple recipe combines just a few ingredients and some savvy cooking techniques for a delicious, elegant dinner.

SERVES: 2 to 4   PREP TIME: 10 minutes   COOK TIME: 35 minutes

4 tablespoons coconut oil, divided

6 to 8 bone-in chicken thighs (about 2 pounds), skin removed

2 cups sliced cremini mushrooms

2 shallots, minced

1 teaspoon fresh thyme leaves

2 tablespoons port

2 tablespoons coconut cream

sea salt to taste

freshly ground pepper to taste

1. Heat the cast iron skillet over medium-high heat until hot, about 2 minutes. Melt 2 tablespoons of the coconut oil in the skillet, tilting to coat the bottom of the pan.

2. Pat the chicken dry with paper towels, and season generously with salt and pepper. Sear on each side for 3 to 4 minutes, until nicely browned. Transfer the chicken to a separate dish. It will not be cooked through.

3. Add another tablespoon of oil to the pan and cook the mushrooms. You will need to do this in a few batches to not crowd the pan. Add more oil as needed.

4. Push the mushrooms to the sides of the pan. Add the shallots and thyme, and cook for about 2 minutes. Transfer the chicken back to the pan, cover, and cook for 20 minutes, until the chicken is cooked through.

5. Remove the chicken to a serving plate. Add the port to the pan and cook until reduced by about half. Stir in the coconut cream, season with salt and pepper, and cook until thick and bubbling, about 2 to 3 more minutes. Ladle the sauce and mushrooms onto the chicken and serve.

RUSTIC CHICKEN POT PIE

As much as I love individual serving portions, there's something wonderful about sharing a dish as a family. Serve directly from the skillet.

SERVES: 2 to 4   PREP TIME: 15 minutes   COOK TIME: 45 minutes

2 cups finely ground, blanched almond flour

2 tablespoons coconut flour

½ teaspoon sea salt

¼ cup palm shortening

1 egg

1 to 2 tablespoons ice water

2 tablespoons coconut oil

6 to 8 boneless chicken thighs (about 2 pounds total), cut into 1-inch chunks

1 yellow onion, minced

4 carrots, diced

4 Yukon Gold potatoes, peeled and cut into 1-inch chunks

3 tablespoons tapioca starch

1 cup chicken broth

1 cup green peas

sea salt to taste

freshly ground pepper to taste

1. Begin by making the crust. Combine the almond flour, coconut flour, and sea salt in a food processor. Add the shortening, egg, and 1 tablespoon of the ice water. Pulse a few times, just until integrated. It should form a ball and pull away from the sides. If not, add the remaining tablespoon of water, 1 teaspoon at a time as needed. Wrap the dough in plastic and place in the refrigerator while you get on with the filling.

2. Preheat the oven to 325°F.

3. Heat the cast iron skillet over medium-high heat until hot, about 2 minutes. Add the coconut oil and tilt the pan to coat.

4. Pat the chicken thighs with paper towels, and season generously with salt and pepper. Cook in the skillet, browning on all sides, for about 10 minutes total. Transfer to a separate dish.

5. Reduce the heat to medium and add the onion. Cook for 5 minutes, until somewhat softened. Add the carrots and potatoes, and cook for another 5 minutes.

6. Add the tapioca starch to the pan and stir to mix until it is nearly dissolved. Add the chicken broth, peas, and cooked chicken. Bring to a simmer then remove from the heat.

7. Roll out the pastry crust between two sheets of parchment paper until it is the size of the skillet. Carefully place it on top of the chicken, pressing gently so that the crust touches the chicken and vegetables. Cut a few slits in the crust.

8. Bake for 25 minutes, until the crust is golden brown and the filling is piping hot. Allow to cool for at least 15 minutes.

CUBAN CHICKEN STEW

This chunky stew comes together easily with pantry staples. It is especially good prepared a day ahead of time to allow the flavors to come together.

SERVES: 4   PREP TIME: 10 minutes   COOK TIME: 35 to 40 minutes

1 tablespoon coconut oil

6 to 8 bone-in chicken thighs (about 2 pounds total), skin removed

2 green bell peppers, cored and thinly sliced

1 yellow onion, halved and thinly sliced

4 to 6 cloves garlic, smashed

2 tablespoons tomato paste

½ cup dry white wine

1 quart chicken broth

2 white sweet potatoes, peeled and diced, about 4 cups total

1 tablespoon fresh oregano

1 teaspoon ground cumin

1 cup peas, frozen and defrosted

2 tablespoons capers, rinsed and drained

2 tablespoons raisins

½ cup pitted green olives

1 lime, halved

sea salt to taste

freshly ground pepper to taste

1. Heat the cast iron skillet over medium-high heat until hot, about 2 minutes. Add the coconut oil and tilt to coat the bottom of the pan.

2. Pat the chicken dry with paper towels and season generously with salt and pepper.

3. Place it into the skillet and brown for about 3 to 4 minutes on each side. Transfer the chicken to a separate dish. It will not be cooked through.

4. Add the bell peppers and onion to the pan, and cook for 5 to 7 minutes, until soft and fragrant. Add the garlic to the pan and cook for 1 minute. Add the tomato paste to the pan and cook until it is slightly caramelized, about 2 minutes.

5. Deglaze the pan with the white wine, scraping the browned bits off of the pan with a wooden spoon. Add the chicken broth, sweet potatoes, oregano, and cumin. Season with salt and pepper and bring to a simmer.

6. Nestle the chicken into the pan, cover, and continue cooking for about 20 minutes, until the chicken is cooked through to an internal temperature of 165°F and the sweet potatoes are soft.

7. Stir in the peas, capers, raisins, and olives, and cook until just heated through. Season with lime juice to taste.

ROASTED CHICKEN WITH SUMAC, WALNUTS, AND GARLIC

Sumac is a spice used in Middle Eastern cuisine. It imparts a sour, lemony flavor and can be used as a garnish or stirred into salad dressings and rice.

SERVES: 2 to 4   PREP TIME: 10 minutes, plus 1 to 8 hours inactive time
COOK TIME: 35 minutes

4 cloves garlic, minced

zest and juice of 1 lemon

2 tablespoons kosher salt

1 tablespoon peppercorns

4 cups water

6 to 8 chicken thighs

1½ tablespoons coconut oil

1 yellow onion, halved and thinly sliced

sea salt to taste

freshly ground pepper to taste

1 tablespoon sumac

2 tablespoons minced toasted walnuts

½ cup roughly chopped fresh cilantro

1. Combine the garlic, lemon zest and juice, salt, peppercorns, and water in a small saucepan. Bring to a simmer and stir until the salt is dissolved. Remove from the heat and cool thoroughly.

2. In a nonreactive dish, toss the chicken thighs in the brine and refrigerate for at least 1 hour or up to 8 hours. Remove the chicken from the brine and pat dry with paper towels. Discard the brine.

3. Preheat the oven to 400°F.

4. Heat the coconut oil in the cast iron skillet over medium-high heat until nearly smoking. Place the chicken skin-side down in the pan and sear for 3 to 4 minutes, or until good and brown. Flip the chicken to the other side. Scatter the onion around the chicken and place the skillet into the oven. Season lightly with salt and pepper.

5. Bake for 30 minutes, or until the chicken is cooked through and the onion is soft.

6. Sprinkle the sumac, walnuts, and cilantro over the chicken and onion just before serving.

CORIANDER-CRUSTED CHICKEN THIGHS WITH MINT AND PEA SALAD

I prefer to grind whole coriander seeds in a mortar and pestle for a coarse and crunchy texture. You can also use a pepper or coffee grinder.

SERVES: 2 to 4   PREP TIME: 5 minutes   COOK TIME: 30 to 35 minutes

2 tablespoons coconut oil

6 to 8 bone-in, skin-on chicken thighs (about 2 pounds total)

1 tablespoon whole coriander seeds, coarsely ground

2 cups peas, frozen and defrosted

1 teaspoon minced fresh ginger

1 tablespoon minced fresh mint

1 teaspoon lemon juice

1 tablespoon extra-virgin olive oil

sea salt to taste

freshly ground pepper to taste

1. Preheat the oven to 400°F.

2. Heat the cast iron skillet over medium-high heat until hot, about 2 minutes. Add the coconut oil and tilt to coat the bottom of the pan.

3. Pat the chicken dry with paper towels, season generously with salt, pepper, and the ground coriander. Place the chicken skin-side down into the skillet and sear for 4 minutes to get a nice brown crust. Flip the chicken onto the other side and transfer to the oven. Cook for 25 to 30 minutes, until the chicken is cooked through to an internal temperature of 165°F and the juices run clear.

4. While the chicken is roasting, prepare the salad. Combine the peas, ginger, mint, lemon juice, and olive oil. Season to taste with salt and pepper. Set aside.

5. Allow the chicken to rest for 5 minutes before serving with the pea and mint salad.

LAOTIAN LARB LETTUCE CUPS

This delicious Southeast Asian recipe for "meat salad" is perfect for a quick summer evening dinner. It also makes excellent leftovers, if by some remote chance you do not finish it in one sitting.

SERVES: 2   PREP TIME: 10 minutes   COOK TIME: 10 minutes

1 tablespoon coconut oil

1 pound boneless, skinless chicken thighs, minced

½ red onion, minced

⅛ teaspoon red chili flakes

1 teaspoon minced ginger

1 clove garlic, minced

2 teaspoons fish sauce

1 tablespoon lime juice

2 green onions, thinly sliced on a bias

handful fresh cilantro, roughly chopped

handful fresh mint leaves, roughly chopped

1 head butter lettuce, leaves rinsed and patted dry

1. Heat the cast iron skillet over medium-high heat until hot, about 2 minutes. Melt the coconut oil in the pan and tilt to coat the bottom of the pan.

2. Sauté the chicken until nearly cooked through and gently browned, about 6 to 8 minutes. Add the red onion, red chili flakes, ginger, and garlic, and cook for 1 minute. Add the fish sauce and lime juice, and cook for another minute.

3. Remove the pan from the heat and stir in the green onions, cilantro, and mint.

4. To serve, scoop the mixture into individual lettuce leaves.

VARIATION: You can swap pork or beef for this recipe measure for measure. Cooking times will vary somewhat.

CHICKEN CASSOULET

Traditional cassoulet is hearty and filling with white beans and a variety of meats, usually duck, goose, pork, and sometimes mutton. Like many classic French dishes—beef bourguignonne and ratatouille, for example—cassoulet is at its roots a peasant dish and should be adaptable to your budget and dietary preference. In this version, I've swapped the beans for extra vegetables. I also use chicken instead of duck because it is easily accessible in most grocery stores.

SERVES: 4 to 6   PREP TIME: 15 minutes   COOK TIME: 2½ to 3 hours

½ pound salt pork, cut into lardons

2 pounds bone-in chicken thighs

1 pound chicken drumsticks

2 garlic sausage links, casings removed and crumbled

1 yellow onion, diced

3 carrots, diced

3 celery stalks, diced

6 cloves garlic, smashed

2 bay leaves

32 ounces chicken broth

¼ cup dry white wine

1 medium white sweet potato, peeled and diced

sea salt to taste

freshly ground pepper to taste

1. Preheat the oven to 425°F.

2. Heat the cast iron skillet over medium heat and cook the salt pork until it renders most of its fat, about 10 minutes. Transfer the cooked pieces of meat to a separate dish.

3. Pat the chicken thighs dry with paper towels and season lightly with salt and pepper. Sear in the rendered pork fat for 10 minutes, until well-browned on both sides. Transfer the chicken thighs to the dish with the salt pork.

4. Pat the drumsticks dry with paper towels and season lightly with salt and pepper. Sear in the rendered pork fat for 10 minutes, until well-browned on all sides. Transfer the drumsticks to the dish with the thighs and salt pork.

5. Add the garlic sausage to the pan and brown for 5 minutes. Push the meat to the side and add the onion, carrots, and celery to the pan. Cook for 5 minutes, until beginning to soften. Add the garlic and bay leaves, and cook for 30 seconds.

6. Pour in the chicken broth and white wine, and bring everything to a simmer. Add the sweet potato and salt pork and stir. Nestle the chicken thighs and legs into the mixture and place the pan into the oven.

7. Roast uncovered for 1½ to 2 hours, until the top is browned and bubbling.

PAN-SEARED DUCK BREAST

I first tasted duck breast while living in England where the meat was at the butcher's counter of every supermarket, even in my small town. The breast meat is tender and ensconced in a thick layer of fat. The cast iron skillet is the best tool for cooking it because it does well with a good sear to render the fat and then finishing in the oven. While the duck is resting, use the rendered duck fat to make the Green Beans with Caramelized Shallots (page 32) for a complete meal.

SERVES: 2   PREP TIME: 5 minutes   COOK TIME: 10 minutes

2 (6-ounce) Muscovy duck breasts

sea salt to taste

freshly ground pepper to taste

1. Preheat the oven to 350°F.

2. Heat the cast iron skillet over medium-high heat until very hot, about 5 minutes.

3. While the pan is heating, score the duck breasts by placing them skin-side up on a cutting board. Make several cuts through the skin in a diamond pattern at about 1 inch apart. Do not cut the meat. Season generously with salt and pepper.

4. When the pan is hot, place the duck skin-side down into the pan. Sear for 5 minutes. Flip the duck and sear for another 2 minutes.

5. Transfer the pan to the oven and cook for another 5 minutes.

6. Remove the duck to a cutting board to rest for a few minutes before slicing at a 45-degree angle.

DUCK CONFIT

This timeless duck preparation method is perfect for elegant dinner parties or for slicing and serving over a simple salad. Make sure to save the duck fat for other uses, such as making omelets or searing chicken.

SERVES: 6   PREP TIME: 5 minutes, plus 24 to 48 hours inactive time
COOK TIME: 2 to 3 hours

6 duck legs with thighs

2 tablespoons sea salt

3 cloves garlic, minced

1 shallot, minced

2 sprigs fresh thyme leaves

1 sprig fresh rosemary, needles only

4 cups duck fat

freshly ground black pepper to taste

1. Place the duck legs in a nonreactive dish and season with the salt, garlic, shallot, thyme, and rosemary. Cover tightly and refrigerate for 24 to 48 hours.

2. Preheat the oven to 225°F.

3. Melt the duck fat in the cast iron skillet over low heat.

4. Brush the seasonings off of the duck. Place the duck into the fat and turn to coat each piece thoroughly.

5. Place the cast iron skillet into the oven and bake uncovered for 2 to 3 hours, until the duck meat easily falls from the bone when pierced with a fork. Season with pepper. Cool for at least 10 minutes before serving.

6. Transfer to an alternative dish to chill and store in the refrigerator.

DUCK A L'ORANGE

This classic mid-century dish makes the perfect holiday centerpiece or special occasion meal. Serve with an array of vegetable side dishes.

SERVES: 2 to 4   PREP TIME: 10 minutes   COOK TIME: 1½ to 2 hours

- 5 to 6 pound Pekin duck (also called Long Island duck)
- 2 tablespoons coconut oil, divided
- 1 yellow onion, cut into wedges
- 2 fresh thyme sprigs
- 2 bay leaves
- 1 leek, halved lengthwise and rinsed thoroughly
- 2 celery stalks
- Zest and juice of 2 oranges
- 1 cup chicken broth
- 1 tablespoon red wine vinegar
- 2 tablespoons maple syrup
- 2 tablespoons Grand Marnier (optional)
- sea salt to taste
- freshly ground pepper to taste

1. Preheat the oven to 425°F.

2. Pat the duck dry with paper towels, coat with 1 tablespoon of the coconut oil, and season inside and out with salt and pepper.

3. Place a few of the onion wedges, 1 sprig of thyme, and 1 bay leaf inside the duck.

4. Spread the remaining onion, thyme, bay leaf, leek, and celery in the cast iron skillet. Drizzle with the remaining tablespoon of coconut oil.

5. Roast for 30 minutes. Reduce the heat to 350°F.

6. Add the orange juice, zest, and chicken broth to the pan. Continue roasting for another 1 to 1½ hours, or until the duck reaches an internal temperature of 170°F.

7. Remove the duck from the pan and set on a cutting board to rest.

8. Remove the cooked vegetables from the skillet and discard. Carefully pour the juices from the pan through a fine-mesh sieve. Scoop off the top layer of fat from the pan juices and save for another use.

9. Return the skillet to the stove and turn the heat to medium-low. Pour 1 cup of the reserved pan juices to the skillet along with the vinegar, maple syrup, and Grand Marnier, if using. Simmer until reduced by half, about 5 to 10 minutes.

10. Serve the duck family-style with the sauce on the side.

CHAPTER EIGHT

Pork

MAPLE ALMOND PORK CHOPS

The sweet and savory brine produces a juicy, delicious pork chop. Thick pork chops are the best, but 12 ounces is a lot of meat for one person. So plan to have extras or to share with fellow diners. While the meat rests, make a quick-cooking vegetable, such as the Green Beans with Caramelized Shallots (page 32) for a complete meal.

SERVES: 2 to 4   PREP TIME: 10 minutes, plus 30 minutes to 1 hour inactive time   COOK TIME: 10 minutes

2 cups unsweetened almond milk

2 tablespoons maple syrup

2 tablespoons kosher salt

1 teaspoon whole peppercorns

1 bay leaf

1 sprig fresh thyme leaves

2 bone-in pork chops (about 12 ounces each)

1 tablespoon coconut oil

1. Whisk the almond milk, maple syrup, salt, peppercorns, bay leaf, and thyme together. Pour it into a shallow, nonreactive baking dish. Place the pork chops into the brine about 30 minutes or up to 1 hour before you plan to cook dinner. Too long will denature the proteins and make the chop mushy.

2. Remove the pork chops and pat dry with a paper towel.

3. Heat the cast iron skillet over medium-high heat until hot. Add the coconut oil and tip the pan to coat it.

4. Sear the pork chops on each side for about 5 minutes. They should be good and brown on each side and reach an internal temperature of 145°F. Remove them to a cutting board and tent with foil for about 5 minutes before serving.

MUSTARD BALSAMIC GLAZED PORK CHOPS

My brother lived in Italy and sent me a selection of balsamic vinegars for my birthday. They were thick, syrupy, and complex—so delicious you could drizzle them over gelato. Fortunately, even everyday balsamic that hasn't been aged becomes sweet and syrupy when it is cooked down. Here it is infused with rosemary and Dijon mustard.

SERVES: 2 to 4   PREP TIME: 10 minutes, plus 1 hour inactive time
COOK TIME: 20 minutes

3 cups water

1 teaspoon black peppercorns

2 tablespoons kosher salt

2 tablespoons coconut palm sugar

1 rosemary sprig, plus 1 teaspoon minced rosemary, divided

2 bone-in pork chops, about 12 ounces each

1 tablespoon coconut oil

½ cup balsamic vinegar

1 tablespoon Dijon mustard

1. Bring the water, peppercorns, salt, sugar, and rosemary sprig to a simmer over medium heat in a small saucepan to form a brine. Remove from the heat and allow to cool completely.

2. In a shallow baking dish, pour the brine over the pork chops and allow to soak for at least 1 hour.

3. Remove the pork chops from the brine and pat dry with paper towels.

4. Heat the cast iron skillet over medium-high heat until hot. Add the coconut oil and tip the pan to coat it.

5. Sear the pork chops on each side for about 5 minutes. They should be good and brown on each side and reach an internal temperature of 145°F. Remove them to a cutting board and tent with foil for about 5 minutes while you make the glaze.

6. In the same skillet, add the balsamic vinegar, mustard, and remaining teaspoon of rosemary. Simmer for about 10 minutes, or until reduced by about half. Drizzle the glaze over each of the pork chops and serve immediately.

COOKING TIP: Brining is the key to moist and delicious pork chops. Use this basic brine for all of your pork chop recipes to ensure amazing and consistent results.

PORK MARSALA WITH MUSHROOMS

Put dinner on the table in a flash with this delicious pork and mushroom dish. Typical marsala dishes are thickened with wheat flour, but here I use potato starch. You can also use tapioca starch if you avoid potato, but the result has a slightly gummy texture.

SERVES: 4   PREP TIME: 10 minutes   COOK TIME: 20 minutes

1 tablespoon coconut oil

4 boneless, center-cut pork chops

sea salt to taste

freshly ground pepper to taste

2 tablespoons potato starch

2 shallots, sliced lengthwise

2 cups sliced cremini mushrooms

2 large cloves garlic, minced

1 teaspoon fresh thyme leaves

¼ cup marsala

½ cup chicken broth

1. Heat the cast iron skillet over medium-high heat until hot, about 2 minutes. Melt the coconut oil and tilt to coat the bottom of the pan.

2. Season the pork chops generously with salt and pepper, and coat lightly in the potato starch, shaking off any excess. Sear the pork chops for 3 to 4 minutes on each side, until browned, then transfer to a cutting board.

3. In the same pan, cook the shallots, mushrooms, garlic, and thyme for 4 to 5 minutes, until soft. Deglaze the pan with marsala, scraping up the browned bits off the bottom of the pan.

4. Add the chicken broth and bring to a simmer. Return the pork chops to the pan, cover, and cook for 8 to 10 minutes until the pork is cooked through and the mushroom mixture is thick.

GARLIC AND ROSEMARY PORK TENDERLOIN

Pork tenderloin does well with a good sear on the stove and then finishing in the oven. This recipe is perfect as a dinner for two with leftovers for a big lunch over salad the next day. Serve it with a parsnip puree or mashed sweet potatoes.

SERVES: 2 to 4   PREP TIME: 5 minutes, plus 30 minutes to 8 hours inactive time   COOK TIME: 1 hour 10 minutes

sea salt to taste

freshly ground pepper to taste

1 tablespoon minced garlic

1 tablespoon minced fresh rosemary

1 tablespoon olive oil

1½ to 2 pounds pork tenderloin

1. Combine the sea salt, pepper, garlic, rosemary, and olive oil in a small mixing bowl. Pour this mixture over the pork, cover, and refrigerate for at least half an hour or up to 8 hours.

2. Preheat the oven to 325°F.

3. Heat the cast iron skillet over medium-high heat until hot, about 2 minutes.

4. Pat the pork dry with paper towels. Place it into the skillet and brown on all sides, about 10 minutes total. Transfer to the oven and roast uncovered for about 1 hour, until it reaches an internal temperature of 145°F.

SWEET AND SPICY PULLED PORK

There are as many recipes for pulled pork as there are Southern cooks. This version is as simple as they come and uses Paleo ingredients for a filling, hearty main course. Serve topped with a simple cumin-scented coleslaw. The preparation and cooking time is long but almost completely hands off.

SERVES: 6 to 8   PREP TIME: 10 minutes, plus 12 hours inactive time
COOK TIME: 6 to 8 hours

2 tablespoons maple syrup

½ cup sea salt or kosher salt, plus more for seasoning

1 tablespoon peppercorns

2 quarts water

6 pounds bone-in pork butt, also called pork shoulder roast

1 tablespoon coconut oil

2 yellow onions, cut into thick rings

8 cloves garlic

2 tablespoons smoked paprika

2 tablespoons ground cumin

½ teaspoon ground cayenne pepper

¼ cup tomato paste

2 tablespoons red wine vinegar

2 tablespoons maple syrup

freshly ground black pepper

1. To make the brine, combine the maple syrup, salt, peppercorns, and water in a large sealable container, such as a zip-top bag or a ceramic baking dish. Coat the pork butt in the brine and refrigerate for 12 hours.

2. When the pork has finished brining, preheat the oven to 300°F. Coat the cast iron skillet with 1 tablespoon of the coconut oil.

3. Spread the onion rings and garlic cloves in the skillet.

4. Remove the pork from the brine and pat dry with paper towels.

5. Mix the paprika, cumin, and cayenne pepper together, and pat them onto the pork. Cover and roast for 6 to 8 hours, or until the pork reaches an internal temperature of 200°F and is falling off the bone. Remove the pork to a cutting board and allow to rest.

6. Add the tomato paste, red wine vinegar, and maple syrup to the onion and garlic mixture. Stir to combine. Shred the meat with two forks and fold it into the onion mixture and season to taste with salt and pepper before serving.

SAGE ROASTED PORK BELLY WITH STEWED GREENS

Pork belly does best with a long, slow cooking time to produce a meltingly tender texture followed by an intense blast of heat to crisp up the skin. Quickly stew a bunch of dark leafy greens in the rendered pork fat and add a hint of sweetness from dried plums.

SERVES: 4 to 6   PREP TIME: 10 minutes   COOK TIME: 3 hours

2 to 3 pounds pork belly

1 tablespoon coconut oil

1 tablespoon minced fresh sage

1 teaspoon coarse sea salt, plus more for seasoning

1 shallot, minced

2 tablespoons minced dried plums

2 bunches mustard greens, roughly chopped

1 cup chicken broth

1 teaspoon apple cider vinegar

freshly ground black pepper to taste

1. Preheat the oven to 350°F.

2. Score the pork belly with a very sharp knife, or have your butcher do this for you. Rub it with the coconut oil and season with the sage and sea salt. Place the pork belly into the cast iron skillet and place the pan into the oven. Roast uncovered for 2 hours.

3. Increase the heat to 425°F and roast for another 30 minutes. Remove the pan from the oven and carefully transfer the pork belly to a cutting board to rest for 15 minutes.

4. Turn the heat to medium under the cast iron skillet. Cook the shallot and plums in the rendered pork fat for 2 to 3 minutes, until soft. Add the mustard greens, chicken broth, and apple cider vinegar. Cook until soft, about 10 to 12 minutes. Adjust seasoning with salt and pepper.

5. Slice the pork belly and serve a few slices atop the stewed greens.

SAUSAGE AND ONION STUFFED SWEET POTATOES

I really wanted to create a vegetarian recipe for stuffed sweet potatoes, but sausage was calling to me. So here it is in the pork chapter.

SERVES: 2 to 4   PREP TIME: 10 minutes   COOK TIME: 45 minutes to 1 hour

4 sweet potatoes, pricked all over with a fork

2 tablespoons extra-virgin olive oil

1 yellow onion, halved and thinly sliced

sea salt to taste

2 hot Italian sausage links, casings removed, crumbled

½ cup roughly chopped fresh basil

2 cloves garlic, minced

½ cup canned or fresh diced tomatoes

½ cup Paleo-friendly barbecue sauce

1. Preheat the oven to 400°F. Place the sweet potatoes directly on the oven rack or onto a sheet pan, and bake for 25 minutes, until soft but not mushy. Remove the sweet potatoes to a cooling rack.

2. Meanwhile, heat the olive oil in the cast iron skillet over medium heat. Cook the onion with a generous pinch of sea salt for 15 to 20 minutes, until very soft and browned. Push the cooked onion to the sides of the pan and increase the heat to medium-high.

3. Add the crumbled sausage to the skillet and cook until browned, about 5 minutes. Remove the pan from the heat. Transfer the cooked onion and sausage to a large mixing bowl. Wipe the pan somewhat clean with a paper towel.

4. When cool enough to handle, slice the sweet potatoes lengthwise and scoop out the flesh, being careful not to break the skins. Add the cooked sweet potato to the onion and sausage mixture.

5. Stir in the basil, garlic, diced tomatoes, and barbecue sauce. Mix thoroughly.

6. Arrange the sweet potato skins in the cast iron skillet and fill each with the sausage and onion mixture. Transfer the pan to the oven and bake for 15 minutes, until the tops are gently browned.

SWEDISH MEATBALLS

This is the perfect meal for winter or late fall, or it makes a fine New Year's Eve meal with a steaming mug of glogg.

SERVES: 2 to 4   PREP TIME: 10 minutes   COOK TIME: 45 minutes

2 tablespoons coconut oil, divided

1 small yellow onion, minced

1 pound ground pork

½ pound ground beef

2 egg yolks

½ teaspoon sea salt, plus more for seasoning

¼ teaspoon ground allspice

¼ teaspoon ground nutmeg

1 teaspoon minced garlic

2 tablespoons tapioca starch

2 cups beef broth

3 tablespoons coconut cream

freshly ground black pepper to taste

1. Preheat the oven to 325°F.

2. Melt 1 tablespoon of the coconut oil in the cast iron skillet and cook the onion with a pinch of sea salt until soft, 5 to 7 minutes.

3. Transfer the onion to a large mixing bowl and add the pork, beef, egg yolks, sea salt, allspice, nutmeg, and garlic. Use your hands to mix thoroughly.

4. Form the meat mixture into about 2 dozen small balls. Add the remaining tablespoon of oil to the cast iron skillet as needed. Fry the meatballs in batches, browning on all sides, about 10 minutes per batch. Transfer the cooked meatballs to a heat-proof dish and place in the warmed oven.

5. When all of the meatballs are done cooking, add the tapioca starch to the pan and whisk to coat it in the oil. Add the beef broth, and whisk thoroughly to scrape up the browned bits off the bottom of the pan. Bring to a simmer and cook until thick and slightly reduced, about 5 minutes. Whisk in the coconut cream. Adjust seasoning with salt and pepper.

6. Return the meatballs to the pan and serve family-style directly from the skillet.

KALE CARBONARA

I adore the luscious texture and flavor of good pasta carbonara. But after saying goodbye to grain and dairy, it was a distant memory. This kale carbonara has all of the flavors of the original without the wheat.

SERVES: 2   PREP TIME: 5 minutes   COOK TIME: 15 to 20 minutes

4 slices applewood-smoked bacon, cut into lardons

1 bunch lacinato kale, cut into ribbons

2 egg yolks, whisked

1 teaspoon lemon juice

1 teaspoon minced garlic

sea salt to taste

freshly ground pepper to taste

1. Cook the bacon in the cast iron skillet over medium-low heat until it has rendered most of its fat, about 10 minutes. Remove the cooked bacon with a slotted spoon to a separate dish.

2. Add the kale to the pan and cook for 5 to 10 minutes, until bright green and wilted but not mushy. Remove the pan from the heat.

3. Whisk the egg yolks, lemon juice, and garlic together in a large mixing bowl. Add the hot kale and cooked bacon to the bowl and toss quickly to gently cook the egg yolk. Season with salt and pepper.

LEMONGRASS PORK SLIDERS WITH SHREDDED CABBAGE

Lemongrass is an essential ingredient in Southeast Asian cooking and brings a delicious flare to these pork sliders. You can find lemongrass in the produce section whole or already processed as a paste in the refrigerated section. If you use the paste, decrease the amount to 2 teaspoons.

SERVES: 2 to 4   PREP TIME: 10 minutes   COOK TIME: 10 minutes

1 tablespoon coconut oil

1 tablespoon minced lemongrass

1 tablespoon minced ginger

1 tablespoon minced garlic

⅛ teaspoon red chili flakes

1 pound ground pork

sea salt to taste

freshly ground pepper to taste

¼ cup Paleo-friendly mayonnaise

zest and juice of 1 lime

pinch cayenne pepper

2 cups finely shredded Savoy cabbage

½ cup loosely packed fresh cilantro leaves

1. Heat the coconut oil in the cast iron skillet over medium heat. Cook the lemongrass, ginger, garlic, and red chili flakes for 2 to 3 minutes, until fragrant and barely softened. Remove it from the skillet with a slotted spoon to a mixing bowl.

2. Add the ground pork to the mixing bowl, season with salt and pepper, and use your hands to combine everything. Shape the mixture into small patties.

3. Sear the patties on each side for 3 to 5 minutes, or until browned and cooked through.

4. Whisk together the mayonnaise, lime zest, lime juice, and cayenne pepper, and drizzle over each of the sliders, then top with the shredded cabbage and cilantro to serve.

INGREDIENT TIP: To process the lemongrass, remove the tough outer layers and cut away the root end and all but the 2 to 3 inches of the stem end. Use a sharp chef's knife to cut perpendicular to the lemongrass. This eliminates its slivered quality.

CHAPTER NINE

Beef & Lamb

STEAK AU POIVRE

Swap the heavy cream and butter in this traditional French dish with coconut cream for a decadent and flavorful sauce without the dairy. It's delicious with mashed cauliflower or oven-roasted sweet potatoes.

SERVES: 4   PREP TIME: 5 minutes   COOK TIME: 10 minutes

4 (6- to 8-inch) tenderloin steaks

2 tablespoons peppercorns

1 tablespoon coconut oil

2 shallots, minced

⅓ cup cognac or brandy

½ cup coconut cream

sea salt to taste

freshly ground black pepper to taste

1. Season the steaks with salt. Bash the peppercorns in a mortar and pestle until coarsely ground. Press them into the steaks. You can do this a day in advance if you wish.

2. Heat the cast iron skillet over medium-high heat until hot. Add the coconut oil and coat the bottom of the pan.

3. Sear the steaks on each side for about 3 minutes. You may need to do this in two batches to avoid crowding the pan.

4. Transfer the steaks to a serving platter.

5. Reduce the heat to medium-low. Add the shallots to the pan. Cook until slightly softened, about 5 minutes.

6. Carefully add the cognac to the pan, being careful in case it ignites. Simmer until it is reduced to a couple of tablespoons. Add the coconut cream and cook for 1 to 2 minutes. Season the sauce with salt and pepper.

INGREDIENT TIP: Either purchase coconut cream or place a can of full-fat coconut milk into the refrigerator overnight and scoop the thick layer of cream from the top.

MARINATED STEAK FAJITAS

Steak fajitas can be served on Paleo-friendly wraps or crepes, or in butter lettuce leaves. Definitely load them with fresh guacamole.

SERVES: 2 to 4   PREP TIME: 10 minutes, plus 30 minutes to 8 hours inactive time   COOK TIME: 15 minutes

zest and juice of 2 limes

1 teaspoon sea salt

1 teaspoon minced garlic

½ cup minced fresh cilantro

1 tablespoon ground cumin

1 tablespoon ground chipotle

¼ cup extra-virgin olive oil

1½ pounds skirt steak or flank steak

2 red onions, halved and sliced

2 green bell peppers, cored and thinly sliced

2 red, yellow, or orange bell peppers, cored and thinly sliced

1 head butter lettuce, for serving

1. Make the marinade by combining the lime zest and juice, sea salt, garlic, cilantro, cumin, chipotle, and olive oil. Whisk to combine.

2. Place the steak into a nonreactive dish and pour the marinade over the meat. Allow to rest in the refrigerator for at least 30 minutes or up to 8 hours.

3. Heat the cast iron skillet over medium-high heat until hot, about 2 minutes.

4. Drain the marinade from the meat and gently pat dry. Sear the steak on each side for 3 to 4 minutes for medium rare. Transfer the meat to a cutting board to rest for 10 minutes before serving.

5. Return the skillet to the heat, and sauté the onions and bell peppers until gently browned and beginning to soften. Season with salt and pepper. Remove from the heat.

6. Slice the steak thinly on a bias and toss with the peppers. Serve with the butter lettuce along with the guacamole, recipe below.

GUACAMOLE

YIELD: 1½ cups   PREP TIME: 10 minutes

4 avocados, pitted and diced

1 shallot, minced

1 jalapeño pepper, minced

juice of 1 lime

sea salt to taste

freshly ground pepper to taste

1 plum tomato, diced

2 tablespoons fresh cilantro, minced

1. In a mortar and pestle, combine the avocados, shallot, jalapeño, and lime juice. Mash to combine. Season with salt and pepper.

2. Fold in the diced plum tomato and cilantro.

FLAT IRON STEAKS WITH MUSHROOMS

Because flat iron steaks are naturally marbled, the seasoning in your cast iron skillet will provide more than enough coating to prevent the meat from sticking to the pan. Serve this rich entrée with a simple salad of mixed greens or a large, sliced heirloom tomato.

SERVES: 4   PREP TIME: 5 minutes   COOK TIME: 15 to 20 minutes

4 (6- to 8-ounce) flat iron steaks

sea salt to taste

freshly ground pepper to taste

1 to 2 tablespoons extra-virgin olive oil, if needed

1 pint cremini or button mushrooms, halved

1 shallot, minced

1 clove garlic, minced

1 teaspoon fresh thyme leaves

¼ cup dry red wine

1. Heat the cast iron skillet over medium-high heat until very hot.

2. Season the steaks on all sides with salt and pepper. Sear them for 5 minutes on the first side. Reduce heat to medium and sear for another 3 to 5 minutes on the other side to cook to medium-rare. Remove the steaks to a cutting board to rest.

3. Add the olive oil to the pan if it lacks a good coating of fat. Add the mushrooms, browning on all sides for 2 to 3 minutes. Add the shallot, garlic, and thyme to the pan, and cook for another minute. Pour in the wine and cook until reduced to a thick syrup, about 5 more minutes.

4. Serve the steaks topped with the mushroom mixture.

LAVENDER PEPPERCORN-CRUSTED STEAKS

Allow the steaks to rest at room temperature for 20 minutes before you begin cooking them.

SERVES: 2   PREP TIME: 5 minutes   COOK TIME: 10 minutes

1 tablespoon peppercorns

1 tablespoon lavender buds

1 teaspoon coarse sea salt

2 (6-ounce) beef tenderloin steaks

1 tablespoon coconut oil

1. Preheat the oven to 400°F.

2. Heat the cast iron skillet over medium heat until very hot, about 5 minutes.

3. Combine the peppercorns, lavender, and sea salt in a mortar and pestle or spice grinder and pulse until coarsely ground.

4. Coat the steaks on both sides with the spice mixture.

5. Sear for 3 to 5 minutes on one side to get a good sear. Flip the steak and transfer to the oven to finish for another 5 minutes for medium-rare.

COOKING TIP: Allow the steaks to come to room temperature for at least 20 minutes before placing them into the skillet. This will help them cook more evenly without burning.

MEATBALLS IN RUSTIC MARINARA

It doesn't get any better than meatballs the size of your fist nestled in simmering tomato sauce. This dish stands on its own, but if you want something to twirl around your fork, toss in some spiralized zucchini noodles during the last 5 minutes of cooking.

SERVES: 2 to 4   PREP TIME: 10 minutes   COOK TIME: 45 minutes

1 pound ground beef

½ pound ground pork

1 egg, whisked

1 plum tomato, finely diced

1 red onion, minced, divided

4 cloves garlic, minced, divided

¼ cup minced fresh parsley

1 teaspoon minced fresh thyme leaves

1 tablespoon coconut oil

¼ cup minced button mushrooms

1 (28-ounce) can plum tomatoes, hand crushed

1 (15-ounce) can tomato sauce

¼ cup dry red wine

1 cup hand-torn fresh basil, divided

sea salt to taste

freshly ground pepper to taste

1. Preheat the oven to 375°F.

2. Combine the beef, pork, egg, tomato, ½ of the red onion, 1 of the garlic cloves, parsley, and thyme in a large mixing bowl. Season generously with salt and pepper. Form the meat mixture into 6 to 8 large meatballs. Ideally, allow to rest for 30 minutes at room temperature or longer in the refrigerator before frying.

3. Heat the coconut oil in the cast iron skillet until very hot but not smoking. Sear the meatballs, carefully turning them until browned on all sides. They will not be cooked all the way through.

4. In the same pan, cook the remaining onion, garlic, and mushrooms with a generous pinch of salt for 5 to 7 minutes, until beginning to soften.

5. Add the tomatoes, tomato sauce, wine, and half of the basil, and bring to a gentle simmer.

6. Set the meatballs into the sauce and transfer to the oven. Bake uncovered for 15 minutes, until the meatballs are just cooked through. Do not overcook or they will lose moisture. Sprinkle with the remaining fresh basil.

COOKING TIP: Make sure your pan is well-seasoned before making this recipe; the acidity of the tomatoes can yield a metallic flavor if cooked in an unseasoned pan.

TOMATO ROSEMARY BURGERS

Every Friday night is grill night at my house, but on those occasional days when the weather isn't cooperative, I take burger making indoors. Here's one way to infuse burgers with flavor without the grill.

SERVES: 4   PREP TIME: 5 minutes   COOK TIME: 10 minutes

1 pound ground beef

¼ teaspoon sea salt

½ teaspoon freshly ground pepper

1 tablespoon minced fresh rosemary

1 tablespoon minced sun-dried tomatoes

1 tablespoon minced shallot

8 lettuce leaves, for serving

1 cup Smoky Rosemary Ketchup (recipe follows)

1. Combine the beef, sea salt, pepper, rosemary, sun-dried tomatoes, and shallot in a small mixing bowl. Form into four patties and set aside while you preheat the pan. You can do this several hours in advance if you wish.

2. Preheat the cast iron skillet over medium-high heat, until hot, about 2 minutes.

3. Cook the burgers for 4 to 5 minutes on each side for medium-rare. Serve with lettuce leaves and Rosemary Ketchup.

SMOKY ROSEMARY KETCHUP

YIELD: 1 cup   PREP TIME: 5 minutes

1 cup Paleo-friendly tomato ketchup

1 teaspoon fresh rosemary, minced

1 teaspoon smoked paprika

1 clove garlic, minced

Stir together ketchup, rosemary, paprika, and garlic.

MEATLOAF

This is a meat lover's meatloaf for sure! Instead of bread crumbs or rice to keep the meatloaf tender, use diced tomatoes and mushrooms and top the whole thing with several slices of bacon, which will help seal in the moisture

SERVES: 4 to 6   PREP TIME: 10 minutes   COOK TIME: 60 to 90 minutes

2 tablespoons coconut oil

1 yellow onion, minced

1 red bell pepper, cored and diced

1 cup finely diced button mushrooms

2 cloves garlic, minced

4 plum tomatoes, diced

1 teaspoon fresh thyme leaves

¼ cup minced fresh parsley

1 cup paleo-friendly ketchup

2 eggs, whisked

1 teaspoon sea salt

1 teaspoon freshly ground pepper

1½ pounds ground beef

1 pound ground pork

6 slices bacon

1. Melt the coconut oil in the cast iron skillet over medium heat. Cook the onion and bell pepper until it begins to soften, about 5 minutes. Push them to the sides of the pan.

2. Cook the mushrooms and garlic in the center of the pan for 2 to 3 minutes, until beginning to release their moisture.

3. Use a slotted spoon to transfer all of the vegetables to a mixing bowl. Add the tomatoes, thyme, parsley, ketchup, eggs, salt, and pepper. Stir to mix thoroughly.

4. Add the ground beef and ground pork to the bowl and use your hands to integrate all of the ingredients.

5. Spread the meatloaf into the cast iron skillet and top with the bacon slices. Bake for 1 to 1½ hours until the bacon is browned and has rendered most of its fat and the meatloaf is cooked through. Allow to rest for 10 minutes before serving.

BACON-WRAPPED FILET MIGNON WITH VEGETABLES

I enjoyed the absolute best filet mignon at a little restaurant on the coast of Santa Barbara overlooking the ocean. Perhaps it was especially exquisite because I had just come from the waves and was barely clean enough to be eating there.

SERVES: 2   PREP TIME: 5 minutes   COOK TIME: 20 minutes

2 (8-ounce) beef filet steaks

2 slices bacon

1 tablespoon, plus 2 teaspoons olive oil, divided

1 bunch broccolini

2 carrots, peeled and cut into matchsticks

juice of 1 lemon

sea salt to taste

freshly ground pepper to taste

1. Preheat the oven to 450°F.

2. Heat the cast iron skillet over high medium-heat until hot, about 2 minutes.

3. Wrap each filet in a bacon slice, securing it with a toothpick. Rub each steak with 1 teaspoon of the olive oil and season with salt and pepper.

4. Sear the filets for 2 minutes on the first side. Flip and sear for 1 minute on the second side. Transfer the skillet to the oven and continue cooking for 8 to 10 minutes for medium rare.

5. Carefully transfer the pan back to the stove and remove the steaks to a warmed serving dish to rest for 10 minutes.

6. Add the remaining tablespoon of olive oil and the broccolini to the pan, and sauté over medium-high heat until beginning to soften, about 5 minutes. Add the carrots and cook for another 3 minutes. Season the vegetables with salt and pepper and shower with lemon juice.

7. Serve the steaks with the vegetables on the side.

BRAISED SHORT RIBS

Comfort food doesn't get much more comforting than these succulent braised beef short ribs. Reducing the sauce produces a delicious, thick sauce without the addition of flour.

SERVES: 4   PREP TIME: 10 minutes   COOK TIME: 3 hours

1 tablespoon coconut oil

4 pounds bone-in beef short ribs, cut into 2-inch pieces

sea salt to taste

freshly ground pepper to taste

1 small yellow onion, diced

1 carrot, diced

1 celery stalk, diced

1 tablespoon tomato paste

1 cup dry red wine

2 cups chicken broth

1 teaspoon minced fresh rosemary

1 teaspoon fresh thyme leaves

zest of 1 orange

1. Heat the cast iron skillet over medium-high heat. Melt the coconut oil in the pan and tilt to coat the bottom of the pan.

2. Pat the short ribs dry with paper towels and season generously with salt and pepper. Sear the short ribs on all sides, working in batches so as not to crowd the pan. Transfer them to a separate dish to rest.

3. Add the onion, carrot, and celery to the pan, and cook until soft, 5 to 7 minutes.

4. Stir in the tomato paste and cook for 1 to 2 minutes, until it begins to caramelize. Add the red wine and chicken broth, and bring to a simmer. Add the short ribs to the pan and simmer for 20 to 30 minutes uncovered.

5. Preheat the oven to 350°F while the short ribs cook on the stove top.

6. Stir in the rosemary, thyme, and orange zest, and cover the pan. Transfer to the oven and cook for 2 to 2½ hours, until the short ribs are tender and falling off the bone.

INDIAN BEEF CURRY

This fragrant curry is delicious over riced cauliflower or with Paleo naan bread for sopping up juices.

SERVES: 4   PREP TIME: 10 minutes   COOK TIME: 2½ to 3 hours

1 tablespoon coconut oil

2 pounds beef chuck, cut into 1-inch cubes

sea salt to taste

freshly ground pepper to taste

1 red onion, halved and thinly sliced

4 cloves garlic, smashed

1 tablespoon minced ginger

1 cup diced tomatoes

1 bay leaf

2 tablespoons curry powder

¼ teaspoon ground cinnamon

1 teaspoon ground coriander

½ teaspoon garam masala

1 tablespoon lime juice

1. Heat the cast iron skillet over medium-high heat until hot, about 2 minutes. Melt the coconut oil in the skillet, tilting to coat the bottom of the pan.

2. Pat the beef dry with paper towels and season generously with salt and pepper. Sear the meat in batches, browning on all sides, about 5 to 8 minutes per batch.

3. Transfer the meat to a separate dish. Add the onion, garlic, and ginger to the pan, and cook for 2 minutes. Add the tomatoes, bay leaf, curry powder, cinnamon, coriander, garam masala, and lime juice to the pan. Cook for 1 minute. Return the beef to the skillet and give everything a good stir. Cover and cook over medium-low heat at a gentle simmer until the beef is tender, about 2 to 2½ hours.

THAI BASIL BEEF STIR-FRY

This classic Thai takeout recipe is easy to whip up in just a few minutes. Green beans add more color and volume, but feel free to leave them out for a more traditional dish. Or swap them for broccoli, sugar snap peas, or any other veggie.

SERVES: 2 to 4   PREP TIME: 10 minutes   COOK TIME: 15 minutes

1 pound sirloin tip steak, thinly sliced on a bias

1 tablespoon toasted sesame oil

1 tablespoon tapioca starch

sea salt to taste

freshly ground pepper to taste

2 cups green beans, stems removed

1 red bell pepper, cored and thinly sliced

2 cloves garlic, thinly sliced

1 tablespoon minced ginger

1 small serrano pepper, minced

2 tablespoons fish sauce

juice of 1 lime

1 teaspoon maple syrup

1 cup roughly chopped Thai basil or Italian basil

1. Heat the cast iron skillet over medium-high heat until it is good and hot.

2. Toss the beef with the sesame oil and then sprinkle with the tapioca starch. Season with salt and pepper.

3. Sear the beef in two batches until just browned, about 2 to 3 minutes per batch. Transfer to a separate dish.

4. Add the green beans to the pan and sauté for 2 minutes. Add the bell pepper and sauté for another 5 minutes.

5. Add the garlic, ginger, and serrano pepper to the pan and cook for about 1 minute.

6. Return the beef to the pan. Pour in the fish sauce, lime juice, and maple syrup. Cook for about 1 minute or until thickened.

7. Toss with the basil just before serving.

SPANISH LAMB STEW

Pungent spices are the perfect match for bold-flavored lamb. If you prefer a more sophisticated version, go the French route and try the variation below.

SERVES: 4   PREP TIME: 10 minutes   COOK TIME: 2½ to 3 hours

1 tablespoon coconut oil

2 pounds boneless lamb shoulder, cut into 2-inch cubes

sea salt to taste

freshly ground pepper to taste

1 yellow onion, halved and thinly sliced

2 red bell peppers, cored and thinly sliced

2 garlic cloves, minced

1 teaspoon minced fresh rosemary

⅛ teaspoon cayenne pepper

2 teaspoons smoked paprika

1 tablespoon red wine vinegar

2 cups dry red wine

1. Preheat the oven to 350°F.

2. Heat the cast iron skillet over medium-high heat until hot, about 2 minutes. Add the coconut oil to the skillet and tilt to coat the bottom of the pan.

3. Pat the lamb dry with paper towels and season generously with salt and pepper.

4. Sear the meat in the hot skillet in a few batches, so as not to crowd the pan. Brown on all sides. This will take about 20 minutes total.

5. Add the onion, bell peppers, garlic, rosemary, cayenne pepper, and paprika to the pan. Mix to combine all of the ingredients.

6. Pour in the red wine vinegar and red wine, and stir to pick up any browned bits from the bottom of the pan. Return lamb to pan.

7. Cover the skillet and transfer to the oven. Cook for 1½ to 2 hours, until the lamb is very tender and the vegetables have a sauce-like consistency.

VARIATION: French Lamb Stew

Replace the bell pepper with 4 carrots, cut into 2-inch pieces and 2 turnips, peeled and quartered. Omit the cayenne, paprika, and red wine vinegar. Replace the red wine with ¼ cup dry white wine and 2 cups chicken broth.

CALF LIVER AND ONIONS

When people think of Paleo, this is likely the meal they envision. Organ meats are rich in minerals and an integral part of most modern interpretations of the Paleo diet.

SERVES: 2 to 4   PREP TIME: 5 minutes   COOK TIME: 20 minutes

2 tablespoons bacon fat

2 yellow onions, halved and thinly sliced

1 teaspoon minced fresh rosemary

1 pound calf liver

sea salt to taste

freshly ground pepper to taste

2 tablespoons coconut flour

1. Melt the bacon fat in the cast iron skillet over medium heat.

2. Cook the onions and rosemary with a pinch of salt for 15 minutes, until very soft and the onions begin to caramelize. Push them to the side.

3. Season the liver with salt and pepper and dust lightly with the coconut flour, shaking off any excess. Sear on each side for 3 minutes.

4. Allow the liver to rest briefly before slicing and serving topped with the onions.

CHIMICHURRI LAMB CHOPS

These lamb chops are delicious with Asparagus la Plancha (page 30). They also make great leftovers for serving over a big salad.

SERVES: 2 to 4   PREP TIME: 10 minutes, plus 30 minutes to 8 hours resting time   COOK TIME: 6 minutes

¼ cup red wine vinegar

1 teaspoon sea salt

3 cloves garlic, minced

1 shallot, minced

½ cup minced fresh parsley

¼ cup minced fresh mint

¼ cup extra-virgin olive oil

2 lamb shoulder chops, about 8 ounces each

1. Make the chimichurri by combining the vinegar, sea salt, garlic, shallot, parsley, mint, and olive oil. Whisk to combine.

2. Place the lamb chops into a nonreactive dish and pour the chimichurri over the meat. Allow to rest in the refrigerator for at least 30 minutes or up to 8 hours.

3. Heat the cast iron skillet over medium-high heat until hot, for about 2 minutes.

4. Drain the marinade from the meat and shake away any excess. Sear the lamb on each side for 3 to 4 minutes for medium rare. Allow the meat to rest for 5 minutes before serving.

MOROCCAN LAMB WITH PRESERVED LEMONS

I began making preserved lemons when I moved to California and have been in love with them ever since. They're a cinch to make and keep for a long time in the refrigerator after they've achieved the perfect level of brininess.

SERVES: 6   PREP TIME: 10 minutes, plus up to 12 hours inactive time (optional)   COOK TIME: 1 hour 45 minutes

1 tablespoon ground coriander

1 tablespoon ground cumin

1 tablespoon curry powder

1 tablespoon ground ginger

1 teaspoon sea salt

1 teaspoon freshly ground pepper

1 bone-in leg of lamb, about 6 pounds

1 tablespoon coconut oil

½ preserved lemon, minced (recipe below)

¼ cup minced fresh parsley

2 tablespoons minced fresh mint

2 tablespoons extra-virgin olive oil

1. Preheat the oven to 350°F.

2. Combine the coriander, cumin, curry, ginger, salt, and pepper. Coat the lamb in the coconut oil and then rub the spice mixture all over it. To deepen the flavor, allow the meat to rest in the refrigerator for up to 12 hours.

3. Heat the cast iron skillet over medium-high heat until hot, about 2 minutes.

4. Place the lamb leg into the skillet and brown on all sides, about 10 minutes total.

5. Transfer the skillet to the oven and roast for 1½ hours.

6. While the lamb is cooking, combine the preserved lemon (recipe below), parsley, mint, and olive oil.

7. Allow the lamb to rest for 15 minutes before slicing and serving with the preserved lemon relish.

PRESERVED LEMONS

YIELD: 1 cup   PREP TIME: 10 minutes, plus 5 days inactive time

2 lemons

¼ cup sea salt

1 teaspoon coriander seed

1 teaspoon fennel seed

¼ teaspoon red chili flakes

1. Cut the lemons into wedges lengthwise, leaving the stem end intact.

2. Combine the sea salt, coriander seed, fennel seed, and red chili flakes.

3. Stuff the lemons into a half pint jar, squeezing the juice into the jar as you go. After each lemon, pour in some of the spice mixture. Press the lemons down so that they're submerged in juice.

4. Screw on a clean lid and place in a dark place at room temperature for 5 days or longer. Refrigerate after opening.

CHAPTER TEN

Desserts

PAN-ROASTED PEARS WITH THYME

The pears caramelize beautifully in this rustic yet elegant dessert. Serve it with a scoop of Paleo ice cream for a real treat.

SERVES: 4   PREP TIME: 5 minutes   COOK TIME: 60 minutes

2 tablespoons ghee or coconut oil

4 pears, peeled and halved lengthwise

1 tablespoon fresh thyme leaves

pinch sea salt

2 tablespoons maple syrup

1. Preheat the oven to 325°F.

2. Melt the ghee or oil in the cast-iron skillet over medium heat. Add the pears and thyme, and turn gently to coat in the fat. Season with salt. Place the pan in the oven and roast uncovered, turning the pears occasionally, for 45 minutes. Add the maple syrup and continue roasting until the pears are tender and beginning to brown on the edges, another 10 to 15 minutes.

BERRY COBBLER

Make this cobbler in the summertime when berries are naturally sweet. Or, use frozen berries and increase the cooking time by 15 minutes.

SERVES: 4 to 6   PREP TIME: 10 minutes   COOK TIME: 40 minutes

1 tablespoon coconut oil

4 cups blueberries

4 cups blackberries

2 cups hulled, halved strawberries

2 tablespoons tapioca starch

⅓ cup potato starch

⅓ cup coconut flour

1 teaspoon baking powder

¼ teaspoon baking soda

⅛ teaspoon sea salt

½ cup palm shortening

1 egg

½ cup almond milk

2 tablespoons maple syrup

1 tablespoon vanilla extract

1. Preheat the oven to 350°F.

2. Coat the interior of the cast iron skillet with the coconut oil. If your pan is well-seasoned, you may not need to do this.

3. Combine all the berries in the cast iron skillet and toss with the 2 tablespoons of tapioca starch.

4. In a separate bowl, sift in the potato starch, coconut flour, baking powder, baking soda, and sea salt. Cut in the palm shortening, blending until the mixture looks like coarse sand. Make a well in the center of the ingredients. In a large measuring cup, whisk the egg, almond milk, maple syrup, and vanilla extract. Pour it into the center of the flour and shortening mixture. Stir to mix.

5. Scoop the cobbler topping onto the berries at intervals.

6. Bake uncovered for 40 minutes, or until the top is browned and the berries are bubbling.

INGREDIENT TIP: Potato starch offers a generous dose of resistant starch. However, if you're opposed to potatoes, you can use tapioca starch in the cobbler topping.

PINEAPPLE UPSIDE-DOWN CAKE

The pineapple caramelizes beautifully in the cast iron skillet. The pan is heavy, however, so make sure it is completely cool before you invert the cake onto a serving platter.

SERVES: 4   PREP TIME: 15 minutes   COOK TIME: 20 minutes

2 tablespoons coconut oil

1 small ripe pineapple, peeled, cored, and cut into 1-inch-thick slices

6 tablespoons coconut palm sugar, divided

¼ cup palm shortening

3 eggs

1 teaspoon vanilla extract

⅓ cup potato starch

⅓ cup coconut flour

½ teaspoon baking soda

1 teaspoon baking powder

¼ teaspoon sea salt

⅔ cup almond milk

1 teaspoon lemon juice

1. Preheat the oven to 325°F.

2. Heat the cast iron skillet over medium heat until hot, about 2 minutes. Melt the coconut oil in the skillet and brush up the sides to coat thoroughly.

3. Add the pineapple slices and 2 tablespoons of the coconut palm sugar, turning to coat the pineapple in the sugar. Reduce the heat to low and cook for another 5 minutes while you make the cake batter.

4. Cream the remaining 4 tablespoons of coconut palm sugar with the shortening in a large mixing bowl for 1 to 2 minutes. Add the eggs and vanilla, and beat for another minute, until creamy. Sift in the potato starch, coconut flour, baking soda, baking powder, and sea salt. Stir until just combined. Add the almond milk and lemon juice and stir until thoroughly combined.

5. Spread the batter out over the pineapple and transfer the pan to the oven. Cook for 20 minutes, until the cake is golden brown and puffy.

6. Invert the cake onto a serving platter and slice into wedges.

DISTRESSED PEACH CRUMBLE

During my first trip to the Saturday farmer's market in Santa Barbara, peaches were in season and one vendor offered a big discount on "visually distressed" peaches. The overripe ones make the best desserts, so I bought a few pounds and didn't even need to add any sweetener to them. If your peaches are less sweet, consider stirring in a tablespoon or two of maple syrup or coconut palm sugar.

SERVES: 6   PREP TIME: 10 minutes   COOK TIME: 25 to 30 minutes

8 to 10 very ripe peaches, unpeeled, pitted and cut into 1-inch chunks, juices reserved

4 tablespoons tapioca starch, divided

1 cup finely ground, blanched almond flour

2 tablespoons coconut flour

½ teaspoon sea salt

2 tablespoons coconut palm sugar

¼ cup palm shortening

1 teaspoon vanilla extract

1. Preheat the oven to 325°F.

2. Toss the peaches with 2 tablespoons of the tapioca starch in the cast iron skillet.

3. Combine the remaining 2 tablespoons of tapioca starch with the almond and coconut flours, sea salt, and coconut palm sugar. Add the palm shortening, vanilla extract, and 2 tablespoons of the reserved peach juice and use your fingers to combine.

4. Crumble the mixture over the peaches. Bake uncovered for 25 to 30 minutes, until the peaches are bubbling and top is gently browned.

ZUCCHINI CRUMBLE VARIATION: As strange as it sounds, zucchini also makes a delicious crumble. Sweetened gently, it has the aroma of ripe melons. Use 1½ pounds of zucchini in place of peaches in this recipe.

CARAMELIZED RHUBARB PUDDING CAKE

Rhubarb holds a lot of nostalgia for me because my mom used to make rhubarb crisps when I was growing up and we often had it growing in our backyard. She added strawberries and copious amounts of sugar to offset the tartness of rhubarb. Sea salt also acts to blunt its bitterness, leaving only the floral, herbaceous scent of the vegetable.

SERVES: 6   PREP TIME: 15 minutes   COOK TIME: 30 minutes

2 pounds rhubarb, cut into ½-inch pieces

¾ cup maple syrup, divided

¼ teaspoon, plus a pinch sea salt, divided

4 eggs

¾ cup coconut cream

1 tablespoon vanilla extract

3 tablespoons coconut flour

1. Preheat the oven to 325°F.

2. Combine the rhubarb, ½ cup of the maple syrup, and ¼ teaspoon of sea salt in the cast iron skillet. Bring to a simmer and cook down for about 15 minutes, until mostly soft and syrupy.

3. Meanwhile, separate the eggs into two mixing bowls. Whisk the whites with the remaining pinch of sea salt until glossy and stiff peaks form.

4. Add the remaining ¼ cup of maple syrup, coconut cream, and vanilla extract to the egg yolks and beat until thoroughly mixed, 1 to 2 minutes.

5. Lighten the egg yolk mixture by folding in ⅓ of the egg whites. Add the remaining egg whites and sift in the coconut flour. Fold just until combined.

6. Spread the cake batter over the rhubarb and place the skillet into the oven. Bake for 30 minutes, until the top is golden and set. The bottom of the cake layer will still be deliciously squidgy.

CAST IRON APPLE PIE

My mother-in-law taught me her apple pie recipe the first year I was married and it has remained a staple in my kitchen ever since. This is a Paleo version that rivals the original.

SERVES: 8   PREP TIME: 15 minutes   COOK TIME: 40 minutes

2 cups finely ground, blanched almond flour

2 tablespoons coconut flour

¾ teaspoon sea salt, divided

¼ cup palm shortening

1 egg

1 to 2 tablespoons ice water

2 tablespoons coconut oil

8 to 10 granny smith apples, peeled, cored, and very thinly sliced

¼ cup maple syrup

1 tablespoon ground cinnamon

¼ teaspoon freshly ground nutmeg

1. Begin by making the crust. Combine the almond flour, coconut flour, and ½ teaspoon of the sea salt in a food processor. Add the shortening, egg, and 1 tablespoon of the ice water. Pulse a few times, just until integrated. It should form a ball and pull away from the sides. If not, add the remaining tablespoon of water 1 teaspoon at a time as needed. Wrap the dough in plastic and place in the refrigerator while you get on with the filling.

2. Preheat the oven to 325°F.

3. Generously coat the cast iron skillet in the coconut oil.

4. Add the apples, maple syrup, cinnamon, nutmeg, and remaining ¼ teaspoon of sea salt, and toss gently to mix.

5. Roll out the pastry crust between two sheets of parchment paper until it is the size of the skillet. Remove one sheet of parchment and carefully place it on top of the apples, peeling away the second sheet. Cut a few slits in the crust.

6. Bake for 40 minutes, until the crust is golden brown and the filling is piping hot. Allow to cool for at least 1 hour before serving.

BLACK-BOTTOM CHOCOLATE CAKE

Preheating the cast iron skillet gives the bottom of this cake a thick, crusty layer.

SERVES: 4 to 6   PREP TIME: 5 minutes   COOK TIME: 25 to 28 minutes

1 tablespoon coconut oil

½ cup coconut palm sugar

¼ cup palm shortening

4 eggs

1 tablespoon vanilla extract

1 cup finely ground, blanched almond flour

½ cup cocoa powder

1 teaspoon baking soda

½ teaspoon sea salt

1. Preheat the oven to 325°F.

2. Heat the cast iron skillet over medium heat until hot, about 2 minutes. Coat the bottom and sides with the coconut oil.

3. In a food processor, combine the palm sugar and palm shortening. Blend for 1 minute, scraping down the sides as needed. Add the eggs and vanilla extract, and blend for another minute, again scraping the sides as needed.

4. Add the almond flour, cocoa powder, baking soda, and sea salt. Pulse a few times, scrape down the sides, and then blend just until integrated.

5. Scape the cake batter into the cast iron skillet and place it in the oven. Bake for 25 to 28 minutes, until the cake is set and a toothpick inserted into the center comes out clean. Allow to rest for at least 20 minutes before cutting into slices and serving.

BANANAS FOSTER

This simple dessert deserves a generous scoop of Paleo Vanilla Ice Cream (recipe follows). Or, use these as a decadent topping for Crepes (page 24).

SERVES: 2 to 4   PREP TIME: 5 minutes   COOK TIME: 8 minutes

3 tablespoons ghee or coconut oil

¼ cup maple syrup

¼ teaspoon ground allspice

¼ teaspoon freshly grated nutmeg

¼ teaspoon ground cinnamon

1 teaspoon vanilla extract

2 barely ripe bananas

¼ cup dark rum

1. Melt the ghee or coconut oil in the cast iron skillet over medium heat. Add the maple syrup, allspice, nutmeg, and cinnamon. Cook for 2 to 3 minutes.

2. Stir in the vanilla extract then add the bananas, cut-side down into the pan. Cook until the bananas soften slightly and begin to brown, about 2 minutes on each side. Transfer the bananas to a serving dish.

3. Carefully add the rum to the pan and, if it does not ignite automatically, ignite with a stick match. Continue cooking until the flame dies out, 1 to 2 minutes. Spoon the sauce over the bananas and serve.

PALEO VANILLA ICE CREAM

This is my go-to vanilla ice cream recipe and only takes a few ingredients and less than 10 minutes to prepare. Using almond milk minimizes the coconut flavor, but if you like it, you can use all coconut milk and even fold in toasted coconut just before serving to amplify the flavor.

YIELDS: 5 cups   PREP TIME: 5 minutes, plus 4 hours cooling time   COOK
TIME: 5 minutes

1 (15-ounce) can coconut cream	½ cup maple syrup or coconut palm sugar
2 cups unsweetened almond milk	¼ teaspoon sea salt
	4 egg yolks
	1 tablespoon vanilla extract

1. Heat the coconut cream, almond milk, maple syrup, and sea salt in a medium saucepan over medium-low heat. Remove ½ cup of the heated milk mixture and whisk it into the egg yolks to temper them. Slowly pour the egg mixture back into the pan, whisking constantly.

2. Cook for another 5 minutes, whisking constantly until the mixture reaches about 150°F and coats the back of a spoon. Do not let it get any hotter or it will begin to develop a grainy texture. Stir in the vanilla extract.

3. Pour the mixture into a heat-proof container and top with parchment paper to prevent the cream from forming a skin. Chill for 3 hours until completely cool.

4. Pour the mixture into an ice cream maker and proceed according to the manufacturer's instructions.

5. Transfer the ice cream to the freezer and chill until nearly solid. It is the perfect consistency at about 1 hour. Alternately, chill well in advance and remove from the freezer about 20 minutes before serving.

VARIATION: If you do not have an ice cream maker, pour the mixture from the saucepan into the heat-proof container and place in the freezer uncovered. Stir every hour with a spatula until thick and firm.

CHOCOLATE CHIP SKILLET COOKIE

Chocolate chip cookies are the one dessert that plows through my will power. If I know they're in the house, even in the freezer, they're on my mind. Something about the combination of salty batter and sweet, complex dark chocolate chunks hits the spot. Of course, you can also drop these on a sheet pan and cook them in individual cookies.

SERVES: 8   REP TIME: 10 minutes   COOK TIME: 15 to 18 minutes

⅓ cup plus 1 tablespoon palm shortening, divided

½ cup coconut palm sugar

2 eggs

1 tablespoon vanilla extract

1 tablespoon Kahlua (optional)

2 cups finely ground, blanched almond flour

¼ cup tapioca starch

1 teaspoon baking soda

½ teaspoon sea salt

1½ dark chocolate chunks

Paleo Vanilla Ice Cream (page 154), to serve

1. Preheat the oven to 350°F. Coat the cast iron skillet with 1 table-spoon of the palm shortening.

2. Combine the rest of the palm shortening and coconut palm sugar in a food processor. Blend for 2 minutes, scraping down the sides as needed. Add the eggs, vanilla extract, and Kahlua, if using, again scraping down the sides.

3. Add the almond flour, tapioca starch, baking soda, and sea salt. Blend just until incorporated.

4. Fold the chocolate chunks into the batter and then spread it in an even layer in the cast iron skillet. Bake uncovered for 15 to 18 minutes, until the edges are browned and the center is mostly set.

5. Allow to rest for at least 30 minutes before slicing and serving. Or, top with Vanilla Ice Cream and serve directly from the skillet while it's still hot.

SALTED PISTACHIO BLONDIES

Finishing salts in dessert are amazing. They hit your tongue with the perfect balance of salty and sweet, making them simultaneously satisfying and addicting!

SERVES: 8   PREP TIME: 10 minutes   COOK TIME: 15 to 18 minutes

⅓ cup plus 1 tablespoon palm shortening, divided

½ cup coconut palm sugar

2 eggs

1 tablespoon vanilla extract

1½ cups finely ground, blanched almond flour

1 tablespoon coconut flour

¼ teaspoon baking soda

¼ teaspoon fine sea salt

¾ cup shelled pistachios

1 teaspoon coarse sea salt

1. Preheat the oven to 350°F. Coat the cast iron skillet with 1 tablespoon of the palm shortening.

2. Combine the rest of the palm shortening and coconut palm sugar in a food processor. Blend for 2 minutes, scraping down the sides as needed. Add the eggs and vanilla extract, again scraping down the sides.

3. Add the almond flour, coconut flour, baking soda, and fine sea salt. Blend just until incorporated.

4. Fold the pistachios into the batter and then spread it in an even layer in the cast iron skillet. Sprinkle with the coarse sea salt. Bake uncovered for 15 to 18 minutes, until the edges are browned and the center is mostly set.

5. Allow to rest for at least 30 minutes before slicing and serving.

COFFEE HAZELNUT VARIATION: Swap the pistachios for toasted, roughly chopped hazelnuts and add 1 tablespoon ground espresso to the batter.

Conversions

Temperature Conversions	
Fahrenheit (°F)	Celsius (°C)
325°F	165°C
350°F	175°C
375°F	190°C
400°F	200°C
425°F	220°C
450°F	230°C

Volume Conversions		
U.S.	U.S. equivalent	Metric
1 tablespoon (3 teaspoons)	½ fluid ounce	15 milliliters
¼ cup	2 fluid ounces	60 milliliters
⅓ cup	3 fluid ounces	90 milliliters
½ cup	4 fluid ounces	120 milliliters
⅔ cup	5 fluid ounces	150 milliliters
¾ cup	6 fluid ounces	180 milliliters
1 cup	8 fluid ounces	240 milliliters
2 cups	16 fluid ounces	480 milliliters

Weight Conversions	
U.S.	Metric
½ ounce	15 grams
1 ounce	30 grams
2 ounces	60 grams
¼ pound	115 grams
⅓ pound	150 grams
½ pound	225 grams
¾ pound	350 grams
1 pound	450 grams

About the Author

Pamela Ellgen is a food blogger and cookbook author of *Sheet Pan Paleo*, *Microbiome Cookbook*, *Soup & Comfort*, and *Modern Family Table*. She also writes on fitness and nutrition, and her work has appeared on LIVESTRONG, Spinning.com, and the Huffington Post. When she's not in the kitchen, Pamela enjoys surfing, practicing yoga, and playing with her kids. She lives in California with her husband and two children.